Marital Spirituality

Marital Spirituality

The Search for the
Hidden Ground of Love

by

Patrick J. McDonald
Claudette M. McDonald

Paulist Press
New York, N.Y. / Mahwah, N.J.

Unless otherwise indicated, psalms are reprinted from *Psalms Anew* by
Nancy Schreck, OSF, and Maureen Leach, OSF (Winona, MN: St. Mary's
Press, 1986). Scripture quotations are from THE JERUSALEM BIBLE by
Alexander Jones, ed., Copyright © 1966 by Darton, Longman & Todd,
Ltd. and Doubleday, a division of Random House, Inc. Used by permission
of Doubleday, a division of Random House, Inc. [for distribution of this
publication in the United States of America, Canada and the Philippine
Republic] and are taken from THE JERUSALEM BIBLE, published and
copyright 1966, 1967 and 1968 by Darton Longman & Todd Ltd and
Doubleday & Co. Inc., and used by permission of the publishers [for distri-
bution of this publication elsewhere than in the United States of America,
Canada and the Philippine Republic].

Cover design by Cynthia Dunne

Library of Congress Cataloging-in-Publication Data

McDonald, Patrick J., 1939–
    Marital spirituality : the search for the hidden ground of love / by
Patrick J. McDonald, Claudette M. McDonald.
        p.   cm.
    Includes bibliographical references.
    ISBN 0-8091-3891-3 (alk. paper)
        1. Spouses—Religious life.   2. Marriage—Religious aspects—
Christianity. I. McDonald, Claudette M., 1948–   . II. Title.
BV4596.M3M44 1999
248.8′44—dc21   99-39713
                                                                                CIP

Published by Paulist Press
997 Macarthur Boulevard
Mahwah, New Jersey 07430

www.paulistpress.com

Printed and bound in the
United States of America

Table of Contents

Dedication—

To all our married friends, who taste the hunger for God and dialogue about it seriously, during both light and dark times.

To our deceased married friends, who now find their hunger satisfied and live their dialogue in a ground of love suffused by light never ending.

Acknowledgment—

Our thanks to Maria Maggi, our editor at Paulist Press. Her honesty, support and genuine love for us encourage us to continue to write.

A Note about Scripture Quotes

Apt scripture quotes are especially problematic in a book that focuses on the intricacies of married life, for texts that are not gender inclusive can alienate one or both spouses. Moreover, it is not appropriate for authors to casually paraphrase linguistically sound texts into an inclusive mode.

After much discussion about the need for consistency, accuracy and textual integrity, we decided to restrict ourselves to two sources: The Jerusalem Bible (Garden City, N.Y.: Doubleday, 1966) and Nancy Schreck, O.S.F. and Maureen Leach, O.S.F., *The Psalms Anew: In Inclusive Language* (Winona, Minn.: St. Mary's Press, 1986). The Jerusalem Bible is abbreviated in the text as JB only when the translation is used for a psalm not taken from *The Psalms Anew*.

We realize that while some language problems remain, we invite our readers to exercise patience and create an inclusive mode that is appropriate to their needs.

Introduction

The hidden ground of love lies just beneath the surface of a marriage, where it awaits an invitation to come to life. Like the germination of new seedlings under the soothing warmth of springtime sun, it forms the fertile context for renewed intimacy.

It emerges as the most authentic manifestation of a marital spirituality. Although deep intimacy and marital spirituality form unique expressions of this ground, they often blossom together.

In a good marriage, the hidden ground is transformed into a familiar landscape, gently confirming the couple in their unique style of interaction. This settled homestead invites a genuine trust of one another, firm hope for a future and confidence in their final destiny.

Even in a marriage that falters, the ground can still be trusted, because the roots of love probe deeper than surface interaction. They transcend changing awarenesses of the joys and demands of marriage or limited visions of a couple's future. At times, this very ground can come to life and surprise a couple regarding how solid their marriage can be.

The first taste of the hidden ground of love happens in breathless moments when young lovers sense the beauty in one another for the first time. Powerful feelings of romance, penetrating connections of the heart, endless days and long nights of passion engender a love that is all-consuming.

Excitement, optimism and a captivating presence to one another awaken a couple to their new identity. This identity persists as long as their hearts beat, driving them to cultivate the ideal of love they sensed in the first blush of romance. The development of a mature love is the work of two lifetimes.

Even though the hidden ground of love fosters a distinct array of personal responses, in every one of them the couple turns over a rich topsoil of resourcefulness they never knew existed. Energy seems to come to them from out of the unexplored depths of their persons. Creative vitality invites them to reach more deeply into a reservoir of latent responses and to renew them. Some couples totally reinvent their experience of marriage.

Many spouses cultivate this ground of love by simply learning to love one another more honestly. They redefine the ways they treat one another and open up a marriage that is deeply intimate and richly rewarding.

Others respond to the call of love by developing the fertile realm of a spirituality. This becomes the greatest gift in their marriage, for their love brings them into a romance with the sacred. Not only does all of life become a sacrament, so does their marriage: a lived concretization of the mystery of love.

Some couples discover that the shared quest for a spirituality leads them to explore the bottomless strata of the ground of love, and in its ultimate bedrock layer they find a relationship with the God of love.

God becomes the focus of their hunger, the center of their interaction, their most engaging awareness, the very ground of their being. Even though their interaction is shot through with a genuine intimacy with God, their deepest experience of God is in their discovery that the hidden ground of love is

LOVE ITSELF, the God of compassion, made visible and concrete in everyday life.

For some couples, the discovery of the foundations for their love comes as gently as new seedlings pushing to the surface of damp ground, seeming to appear overnight, as if from nowhere. In these marriages, growth is peaceful and tranquil.

For others, it is like a new island unexpectedly emerging from the floor of the sea, thrusting its way toward the darkened sky with a raw power that alters an entire ecosystem. New ground emerges explosively from the unexplored regions of a changing relationship, leaving the couple breathless and in awe about a bond between them that refuses to be broken.

This book is an exploration of the hidden ground of love and what that ground promises for a marriage. We invite you to explore the nature of this ground with us and to cultivate the fertile soil of a mature, intimate life together.

We have dialogued with couples for a long period of time about what marriage is, how it grows, and especially how to develop what we call a "good marriage." We find that those who enjoy a successful married life have learned to access the rich ground of love, and it seems to be available to them whenever they desire to explore it. For many of them the quest for a good marriage easily opens out into a lived spirituality. They see a healthy marriage and a vital spirituality as one and the same.

We live in an era of renewed interest in the subject of marital spirituality, so we spend much of our time helping couples define what they mean by this phrase. We often describe it as the *search for the hidden ground of love*.

We have combined several elements in this book. Like the old wedding adage, "something old and something new," we combine the New Testament ideal (total transformation in love) with contemporary marital process. We also explore both old and new prayer forms by suggesting ways to bring them into a couple's efforts to develop a married spirituality.

Central to this effort is a reworking of the ancient practice of *Lectio Divina*. Although this name may not be familiar to married couples, *Lectio Divina* is a spiritual practice, developed and refined over centuries in the monastic life. It invites the scriptures to teach, mold and direct us regarding the intricacies of the hidden ground of love. It generally involves a slow, reflective reading of sacred texts, then invites the reader to incorporate their many layers of meaning into a richer experience of life. For couples, this implies a sharing of souls.

The scriptures teach clearly what a couple might sense intuitively about God: God is the deepest ground of their love. They invite a couple to give form, definition, substance and being to what they so often hunger for in a marriage.

Fostering more than an intellectual understanding of love, the scriptures invite a couple to enter into communion with the personal God. This God knows the ways of love and passionately desires to explore its unseen realities with you. God takes a special delight in knowing you love one another, and promises riches that know no limit to those who open themselves up to the mystery of love.

Allow us to explore with you marital spirituality as the search for the hidden ground of love. The exploration will certainly enrich your encounters with one another. If you desire it, your love will open up to continuing encounters with God. We trust the end result of our efforts is an enjoyable guidebook for your search.

Chapter 1: Awakenings

There is no better way to begin an exploration of the hidden ground of love than to tell a love story.

"Come with me into the backyard," Jim invites.

"The backyard, Jim? Why the backyard?" Shana asks.

Her question carries within it layers of skepticism and disappointment associated with other anniversaries gone unnoticed, too many nights of crying herself to sleep.

"You heard me, Shana," Jim repeats gently, "the backyard. I have something I wanna show you. After all, it's our anniversary."

"At least you remembered the date this year," she says dryly, tugging several times at the left sleeve of her sweater until it settles over her shoulders.

"Come on," Jim insists, "it's a nice October evening. Your castle awaits."

Shana walks in silence beside him as they leave the shelter of their suburban two-story, padding their way across the damp grass, still green in the prefrost evening moonlight. She fights back tears of doubt and emptiness, too curious about Jim's intentions to refuse his invitation. Waves of anger tug at her. She knows better than to allow the first stirrings of vulnerability to come to life for fear of another disappointment.

She gave up her dreams of romance in their fifth year of marriage. By their tenth year, she resigned herself to a marriage of mediocrity, focusing on little more than their children's lives and occasional family vacations. On this, the beginning of their nineteenth year, she is numb, resigned to stay in the marriage until the children are on their own.

They stop to rest in the thick dark shadow cast by their privacy fence. Facing them, not ten feet away, in the twilight zone between bright moonlight and dark border, is a domed tent. It is pitched and ready for occupancy, and it glows from within.

"Here," Jim says with a sweeping gesture toward the tent, "look, it's yours. Happy anniversary."

The light invites them both to step inside. Shana, unable to say anything, stoops slightly to enter first. The tent opens warm and cavernous, yielding enough headroom for both of them to explore their new surroundings at full height. Centered in the oval of yellow light from the hanging lantern rests a folding table set in some detail with a casual mix of Shana's best service and everyday warming dishes.

Smells of barbecued chicken, spicy potato salad and sulfur from Jim's slightly theatrical candle lighting invite Shana to relax. He pulls a canvas camping chair away from the table, gesturing for her to sit down.

"Happy anniversary, Shana," he says again.

Shana says nothing, struggling visibly to hold back her tears.

"A tent, Jim?" she says at last. "A tent? I can't believe it; a tent. I've been asking you for this since we got married. I can't believe it. Is this for real or not?"

They lower themselves tentatively into the camping chairs, then reach to begin their meal, squarely facing one another.

"I've been thinking a lot about us, Shana."

"This time, Jim, I'm going to listen and let you do the talking."

"I know, Shana...I've made a lot of mistakes. I know I have not been the romantic guy you dreamed about all these years. I'm really sorry, Shana. I don't want you to divorce me. I ask your forgiveness and another chance to get it right. I don't want to lose you."

She struggles to find an answer to his proposition, makes a few efforts to say something, then chokes up, her tears glistening in the candlelight. Nothing comes.

"I want another chance, Shana. I don't want you to walk out of my life. I've been doing a lot of thinking."

"Yes?"

"I think we can rebuild this marriage. I've changed. I've even been praying to God to help me—us."

Shana's cool exterior masks her anger. She maintains a polite distance, listening to Jim's plaintive monologue. She has been disappointed too many times before; tonight she'll wait and see. She cannot handle one more vain promise.

Time drags on as they eat in silence. They grow sleepy under the spell of a good meal, fine wine and the clear night sky; then Jim announces that he wants to pray. Shana catches her breath. Never once in their entire history has he taken the initiative to address her spiritual hunger.

"Forgive me for not saying yes more quickly, Jim, but I can't quite deal with all this. Tonight's a bit strong. I'm not too sure what to expect anymore. I can't pray...OK? But go ahead; I'll listen to you."

Jim searches for an internal anchor by shrugging his broad shoulders twice, then settles his body around an imaginary center.

"Please God," he says, "help us. I know you've helped me to see things differently. Help Shana hear me. Let me pray for her because she finds this difficult. God—put your arms around us and embrace us. Melt our icy cold hearts and help us to uh...find love again. Help me love Shana in the way she needs to be loved. Amen."

Shana pays little attention to Jim's vocabulary. Instead, she watches his eyes for a sign of the honesty that defines his core. She knows his efforts are for real. She feels nothing for the moment, but within her soul she experiences a quickening, a Presence, but she refuses to let the shift touch her emotions.

She says nothing. They both remain quiet for a long time.

"Would you like to spend the night here?"

"Ye...aah. OK, Jim."

They zip themselves into separate sleeping bags. Jim kisses her politely on her forehead before she rolls over. He sleeps soundly, while Shana watches the lengthening shadows from the full moon inch their way across the backyard.

Marital Spirituality: The Search for the Hidden Ground of Love

Often, in the midst of great turmoil in a marriage, a couple will search for a trustworthy grounding, even one that has eluded them for years. Their search is often stimulated by an admission that their personal resources have run dry and they can no longer offer one another the love they both desire. Their admission of emptiness invites them, sometimes with great tension and fear, to move toward a deeper form of love, which they have implicitly sought in a thousand indirect efforts to tap. As they begin to discover this deeper experience of love, they open up a spirituality.

They sometimes discover the capacity to pray and, in doing so, spade over a rich ground of love that seems to lie just beneath the surface of their relationship. They cultivate this ground in order to bring to life a newness they have never experienced.

This awareness gives them the desired staying power to continue on in the marriage. They do so, discovering an inexhaustible storehouse of love that awakens them to a vision of what their marriage can be. It invites them to open up the rich gratification and sharp challenges love promises. For many couples, this vision carries them toward an encounter with the God of love, and they see God for the first time as source and center of their love.

All spiritualities explore the deeper questions of life, but marital spirituality inevitably carries a couple into the hidden regions of what love promises. We refer to these realities as *the hidden ground of love*. The more they access this love, the more it evolves into the font, foundation and fulfillment of their marriage. It becomes the core of a vital spirituality.

Marital Spirituality and Lectio Divina

In order to offer form and substance to our ideas about opening up the hidden ground of love, allow us to first explore some foundational ideas regarding marital spirituality: how it is founded, how it grows and matures, and what it promises to a couple.

In doing so, we will note some of the characteristics of modern spirituality in general, then discuss the ways that these characteristics offer a special richness to marital spirituality. Our first exploration opens outwardly through the practice of *Lectio Divina*.

We will explain *Lectio Divina* at greater depth as our ideas unfold. For now, we will summarize it. It is an ancient practice of understanding the presence of God among us by dwelling on the riches of the sacred scriptures. It is the art of sacred reading.

Although the ancient practice of *Lectio Divina* seems to be enjoying a renaissance at the present time and is touted as an idea whose time has come, the language, the imagery and the practice itself still appear to be wedded to monastic spirituality.[1]

At best, we find only passing references to *Lectio Divina* as a practice that could somehow bring new life to a marriage.[2] Consequently, almost nothing is written about *Lectio Divina* and its relevance to married spirituality.

Although the passing references are praiseworthy, what is lacking is an examination of how *Lectio Divina* influences, forms and deepens marital process. Our efforts to blend the practice of *Lectio Divina* and marital process will be tentative, but nevertheless the work needs to be done, for we believe it is a viable approach to marriage enrichment. What we will develop in this book finds its origins in our work with married couples in both a private setting and a workshop mode, as well as a twenty-year effort to develop the practice in our own marriage.

In these settings, we have discovered that the blending of something old *(Lectio Divina)* and something new (marital process) offers a solid foundation for couples, and they grasp it quickly. Once *Lectio Divina* is understood and practiced, they find their lives renewed.

These couples discover, in a way that speaks uniquely to them, what the monastic writers claim: *Lectio Divina* is both technique and passion. When done well, it opens up to become a believable form of prayer. It is also a pathway that opens the heart to a grounding in God.[3] As we often say to our couples, "In marriage, *Lectio Divina* is a direct route into the rich treasures of the hidden ground of love."

St. John, the author of the Fourth Gospel, tells us that God cannot be seen, but we can know God by loving one another (1 Jn 4:12–14). The more we learn the way of love, the deeper we sink our roots into its sacred mystery.

Lectio Divina opens the mystery of God's love to us, teaches us how to nurture it, invites us to deepen it and fills us with its power. It invites us to enter into the secret regions of love by opening our hearts and minds to know what we cannot know through our own unaided explorations.

God becomes the teacher, inviting us to enter the realm where God lives. We learn about love because God engages us in an immediate encounter, and this encounter with Love transforms the ways a couple loves one another.

Michael Casey, an Australian Trappist monk, makes the case that sacred reading *(Lectio Divina)* calls forth from us a gradual awakening to the deeper truths of our existence. That implies an interior process, a breaking down of the barriers that impede us from fully grasping the truths of our life. Thus, the practitioner of *Lectio Divina* must move to a level that is deeper, more challenging and even foreign to where they live most of the time.[4]

We believe that this dynamic is similar to what unfolds in a good marriage, as couples wrestle with both the challenges and the joys of love. Love calls them to a sometimes gut-wrenching examination of every one of their beliefs. This action brings them to a new level of awareness as well as a new maturity in their interaction. *Lectio Divina* gives focus, direction and enlightenment to a process that is already unfolding in the depths of a marriage. It is light in darkness.

Lectio Divina:
God as Foundation of Love

Allow us to introduce you to *Lectio Divina* a little at a time as this book unfolds. A simple phrase in the Gospel of John opens our awareness to the presence of God:

> The Word was made flesh,
> he lived among us,
> and we saw his glory....
> (Jn 1:14)

The phrase is taken from the opening paragraphs of John's Gospel, where he presents his readers with an image of a God who exists from all eternity. Yet this same God enters into the world as a Word, spoken by God in a selfless outpouring of love. The Word is the person of Jesus. He comes as "a light that shines in the dark, a light that darkness could not overpower" (Jn 1:5).

John's phrase about the Word living among us can be more accurately translated as God "pitching his tent among us." In John's culture, hospitality was not only a high virtue; it was an essential dimension of nomadic Jewish life.

Nights in the desert presented a hostile environment to a traveler, with dangers that ranged from desert cold to sandstorms to roaming bandits who preyed on those who found no shelter for the night. Finding hospitality and rest were not luxuries; they were a matter of survival.

In the shelter of a tent, guests found a flowering of life for the long night ahead. They were safe from danger. They found friends, food and rest, while they awaited the dawn in order to continue their journey in safety. In the Jewish culture, God is uniquely present because God is the God of hospitality.

The image of *tent* does not carry the dramatic impact for us, who live in large and comfortable homes surrounded by the conveniences that make life in our era starkly different from the Jewish culture of long ago. Nevertheless, the image of God pitching a tent and dwelling among us invites us to open up an understanding of a God who seriously enters into our lives, identifies with how we live and becomes personally involved in our efforts to find meaning and fulfillment in everything we do. God becomes one with us by living our lives with us.

A spirituality begins by seriously exploring our connection with God. We enter into the bedrock foundations of love because God first loves us and invites us to stay the night, rest, be refreshed and come to know how love underlies God's gracious hospitality.

Jim and Shana's experience in their tent confronts them with fresh possibilities for their strained relationship. Even though Shana is completely unbalanced by Jim's behavior, she at least listens to him.

John's Gospel is more universal in its scope than Jim and Shana's story, but it conveys to us that the invisible love of God becomes visible as God joins us in a gracious gesture of hospitality.

As we shall explain in greater detail later, the first energy of *Lectio Divina* flows as God speaks directly to us. The scriptures underscore what we already know: we cannot see God directly. Through the enlightenment of *Lectio Divina,* we experience an unfolding of the mystery and magnitude of God's love.

The second energy of *Lectio Divina* is the energy of an honest response to God's graciousness, and this marks the beginning of a lived spirituality. The scriptures present a God who loves us passionately, and this God invites us to love back in a passionate way, both by loving God and loving one another.

Spirituality is the lived experience of this call and response, accented by the differences in our styles of loving.

We speak of God, then, as the hidden ground of love. By speaking in this fashion, we not only describe the deepest dimension of our lives, we also join a centuries-old tradition that invites a spirituality built more on God's initiatives than our own efforts.

Contemporary Spirituality

The central task implied in this interactive view of spirituality, then, is to live out the full implications of love. All life, all growth begin with an awareness of God's unconditional love. Once that notion begins to touch my awareness, I must address its implications for my life.

What are its ramifications for how I see myself and my destiny? How does it influence the way I treat my spouse? How is a personal relationship with God to be opened up? By loving God directly? By loving my wife or husband more selflessly? Does it open by exploring jointly our relationship with God?

Are married couples called upon to face God in their separateness, their *I-ness*, or do they only know God by sharing their love life?

In order to explore these dimensions of a spirituality in a more disciplined fashion, we will take the phrase *marital spirituality* and cut it in half. By doing so, we will look at some of the components of spirituality itself and explore how these components give texture and depth to our modern notions of a spirituality. We will then put the phrase back together and explore the unique dimensions of *marital spirituality*.

There is a great hunger for a spirituality today. The quest has evolved, for good or ill, into a multibillion-dollar industry. Spirituality takes on many forms and promises to deliver a lot to the consumer. It represents a range of human responses, from clear-mindedness and high energy to an encounter with God in darkness and unknowing.

We hear people speak of their desire for a spirituality that touches them where they live: in the complexity, joys and pain of life. They tolerate an explanation of the classic modes of spiritual growth for a time, then press us to translate these modes into something they can understand. They especially hunger for the deeper dimensions to marriage, ones that can give their routine and pressured lives more meaning.

The following characteristics of a *spirituality* are the ones we hear people refer to most often as they respond to the hungers within them to know God.

A Search for Wholeness

Cindy and Tom find themselves adrift and isolated in their tenth year of marriage. Their energy is depleted, emptied out by such responsibilities as the rearing of three creative children and paying bills, while at the same time meeting the demands of two professional lives.

Cindy is an attorney who takes primary responsibility for litigation in her law firm. Tom is an accountant, struggling through his fourth year of independent practice.

Several visits with a marital therapist helped them, to a certain extent, face their isolation. They learned to communicate with one another by speaking more clearly about their frustrations. In the final analysis, their communication yielded only a deeper confirmation that they are both tired from the unrelenting demands of life.

After several months of better communication, Cindy and Tom know that their lives have improved in a practical way, but they are still unable to find the love for which they hunger. They still lack a vision for their marriage.

Their lives reflect many of the components of wholeness, but they still do not *feel* whole. Their search for wholeness now leads them out of their closed model of marriage and into a nondenominational community.

Both of them grew up as mainstream Protestants, yet they find the evangelical emphasis too heavy-handed for their liberated and well-educated minds.

The openness of the nondenominational community calls forth from them a new and exciting form of spirituality. They no longer image the world as divided in half between sinners and the elect, nor do they see the world as essentially evil.

They embrace the world as good, and they speak seriously about care and concern for Mother Earth. They have learned to hold all living things in reverence. As they experience the wholeness of reality, they find a new wholeness within themselves.

Their notion of prayer is changing as they move away from prayer as a precise formulation of words, toward an openness that is attentive to the rich themes of life, love and growth. Prayer becomes a matter of quieting down as they ground themselves in the reality of an ever-present God of love.

Two years later, they speak of spirituality as the integrating center of their lives. They are no longer at war with the world, their inner selves and one another. They feel an integration of every dimension of their lives: emotions, thoughts and spirit. In brief, they are beginning to experience a wholeness that becomes the fruition of an engaging spirituality. Consequently, they communicate with one another better than at any time in their history.

Wilkie Au and Noreen Cannon, two contemporary spiritual writers, include in their description of wholeness a real feeling of being worthy. They elevate this feeling of worthiness to the level of feeling in "rare form." This genuine expression of inner harmony allows a spiritual sojourner to deal with life from a position of strength and confidence. An at-oneness with God and the universe invites a unique and fulfilling perspective on life.[5]

Is it any wonder that the quality of wholeness changes an entire perspective on life? Cindy and Tom's continued quest for wholeness will drive their efforts to open up ever new dimensions for their quest. Their quest will also bring their marriage to wholeness.

Grounded on Fathomless Truths

The discovery of deeper truths in Tom and Cindy's lives already sets them upon the solid ground of a spirituality, even as they struggle with the demands of a shared life. They still stretch to come to terms with the hard challenges of life or the gender differences inherent in couple-communication processes.

They struggle to balance out the tasks of parenting with the obligations of professional life. They get as tired as they did two years ago, but the deeper truths of their quest ground them in a soil that is more trustworthy. The hard struggle to find a meaning to the middle years of marriage is within reach because they now share an engaging vision of marriage.

As we so often discover in our work with people, vision underlies all spiritual growth, and this vision flows from deeper truths about people and their destiny. They experience an expansiveness of their awareness, an energy that connects them to life beyond their own limited circle of consciousness. Vision pushes them to identify with realities that are lasting in life and love. They feel they come home to their true identity.

Tom and Cindy, for example, know they are invited into a relationship with all other persons on the planet, and this helps them deal with the mundane of their situation more energetically. They draw energy from their developing capacity to pray without words—knowing they are accessing limitless rivers of energy from a divine source.

A developing social consciousness now allows them to see a vision of their daily work as important, because they are charged with a mission to raise their children to become caring citizens of a global network. The truths they explore about their individual destinies draw them into a more engaging dialogue with one another.

They are dogmatic about their belief that a genuine spirituality is more than simply "feeling good." It is an honest exploration of the deepest truths of life and love: who they are, what their destiny might be, where they belong, and what their obligations are regarding social justice.

They find the exploration of these deeper truths both gratifying and frightening. They rejoice in the discovery of truths that are lasting, while challenging one another to let go of views that are narrow, self-serving and narcissistic.

Nevertheless, they trust their process, for the deepest truths firm up at the times when life seems to be the most disjointed. They find a peacefulness in a discovery of the rich truths that make life productive and rewarding.

Who We Really Are

The reality of who we are is a critical dimension of any spirituality. It is more than a discovery of a successful enterprise, a smoothly working relationship or the shared quest for the good life, for these are all surface matters. A genuine spirituality is grounded upon a richer stratum.

The quest for an authentic spirituality invites the person to explore the fuller, deeper reality of love, and it often leads to an understanding that the real ground of love is God. That discovery is based on an internal authenticity that reflects the emergence of a new self.

Amy had lived for twenty years in a marriage, did her best to be loving and tender, but woke up each morning to an emptiness that refused to leave. She could not count the number of times she tried to make Jack happy, but it never seemed to work.

Their animated exchanges about what they wanted from one another usually ended in a shared sadness, for Jack placed the blame for his unhappiness squarely upon Amy's shoulders. She grew tired of fighting for her legitimacy, but a chronic fatigue inevitably forced her to comply with his demands.

She consulted with others about what to do, and they generally invited her to do some praying and stay patient and loving, reflecting the naive belief that Jack would soften and become a happier person. The strategy yielded no results.

Amy awakened with a jolt the night of her forty-seventh birthday. She was haunted by the dark thought that after all her efforts to make Jack happy, he was still miserable. Time was slipping away, and each tick of the clock served as a nudging wake-up call for her to deal with life more honestly. Jack was no better off than a year ago, her energy was depleted and she found no solace in continued sacrifices that yielded no reward.

While Jack slept away beside her, the realization pressed in on her that she was dying emotionally. She also became aware that Jack's continued criticism of her no longer carried any weight. In the midst of great anxiety, she allowed herself to sustain first thoughts about leaving him.

She began to grow angry at him: for controlling too much of her life, for giving him too much power over her person. Ultimately, she realized she was angry at herself for betraying her deepest desires for creativity.

She had to restrain herself from waking Jack and unloading her anger on him, but better judgment prevailed. She let him blissfully sleep the night away as she firmed up her resolution to do something about her situation. For the first time in twenty years, she felt free. She realized that something new was being born within her, and she liked the feeling. She began to make plans about what to do about her life.

As we so often see, the beginning of an authentic spirituality is grounded upon a surprising discovery of a deeper truth about ourselves. It is a true awakening. The discovery not only opens up a new awareness, it brings about a major change in life. It usually clears the way for an encounter with God that is characterized by a lessening of the burden of guilt and an increase of freedom and spontaneity.

Like Amy, the awakening is expressed in a new self that begins to carry life into new spaces. Although the awakening of the self is primarily a psychological matter that may or may not open up to a personal relationship with God, it becomes the center of who we really are.

This new self is like a rock that grounds the person in the deepest truths about their worth, their existence, their value. The theoreticians speak of an internal structure that the person can trust. Self-esteem, a healthy sense of direction and a feeling of well-being are qualities that reflect a newfound wholeness.[6]

We believe that the opening up of a new self easily points toward an encounter with God. The experience of God becomes clearer as an individual clarifies what he or she really wants. As spirituality deepens, it is not unusual that the deepest self is discovered as existing in God. God literally becomes the ground of one's being.

Since the person is essentially a focused *I-ness,* it is difficult to separate psychological realities from spiritual. However, the discovery of the true self is central to any movement of the spirit, for we come to know more of the reality of the unseen God as we discover the truth of our own existence.

Always, a Reflective Process

The love story between Jim and Shana started to come together several weeks after her long, sleepless night in the tent. The products of their reflection were a renewal of not only their individual selves, but a complete reevaluation of their relationship.

Jim had spent most of their marriage sidestepping Shana's efforts to bond. Only once in their nineteen years did he admit his fears of intimacy. Shana found her own difficulties with marriage. Dreams of slipping away to exotic places to enjoy a few refined pleasures were shut down by the demands of rearing four children.

She approximated her visions of space and freedom by cultivating a love of camping, and she frequently asked Jim to buy her a tent of her own. She used every argument she could muster about why it was cheaper to buy than to rent.

Jim bluntly informed her she was crazy to like camping that much. Moreover, he was usually too busy with his growing remodeling company to take weekends away. Shana knew his sidestepping was a stubborn ploy to mask his fears of intimacy. Over the years, the tent became a powerful symbol of closeness, freedom and an openness to life that refused to materialize.

That long night in her new tent, as Jim continued his clumsy but believable efforts to pray, Shana was subtly but surely touched by his honesty. What was obscure and dormant for nineteen years began to stir to life. Several months later, in a conversation with both of them, their reflective processes were clarified.

"At first I thought he was crazy. He had never prayed before. But I watched his eyes. I can tell when he's being evasive. This time his efforts were for real. I felt a stirring, but couldn't let go of my anger that night. Too painful."

"It was real all right," Jim says. "I was so shattered by the reality of impending divorce, I could only turn to prayer. I've never been so honest."

"I think his continued patience told me he's for real. He's never been a patient man. I know something inside him changed. It invited me to give him a chance and let myself become vulnerable. In two months of talking, my passion came back."

"We both moved into a lot of dialogue about what had

happened to us. We examined our selves, our lives, our lost vision of marriage."

"We learned to pray—together," Shana says.

"We have both healed so much, and we keep trying. So much has opened up for us."

Their hesitant encounter in Shana's tent eventually yielded a rich harvest of tenderness. It was the beginning event in a serious reflectivity that is still alive for them. As long as they sustain it, they will grow in love.

Often, a Personal God

Reflectivity takes on a different face when spirituality centers on a relationship with the personal God. Indeed, reflectivity examines basic beliefs, significant life situations and deep values, but the important dimension of this process is that it moves to a clearly defined emphasis upon a *relationship* mode.

One friend narrated this story to us as he discovered a new relationship with God through a struggle with a complex life situation.

"I was being compromised too much," he says, "and there was no sensitivity in what the management team was advocating. The only motive was profit, pure and simple, yet my colleagues had the whole thing rationalized as good for the company, good for small-town America, good for our investors.

"I was deeply troubled," he continues. "I could not believe that our aggressively moving into this community would benefit anyone except those who sat at the top of this organization. Sure enough, we could deliver hardware, tires, groceries and services better and faster, all under the overshadowing image of corporate America. What we didn't tell the local community was that money would be pulled out of their microeconomy, several family businesses would die and far too many people would be displaced. I had seen it happen many times before but had ignored the casualties. I was haunted by the faces of the neighborhood people who came to the meeting that evening, asking the city council to bar our company from moving into their community. They were so honest and sincere.

"Their faces haunted me into the night," he continues. "I instinctively reached for the scriptures, as I do at times when I need some sort of direction. I turned to the first part of Matthew's Gospel—the story about Jesus being led off into the wilderness for forty days to be tempted by the devil. I knew that the story is written to give us a glimpse of how Jesus struggled with his sense of faithfulness to the call to live authentically.

"I began to get the message: the lure of power, riches, money and pleasure pulled at the life of Jesus as much—probably more—than it does my own. I read this section over and over, making a comparison of my life with this story.

"I thought and thought that night," he continues. "I knew I was being asked by God to make a choice about how to live my life. I shut the New Testament and just flat out asked God to help me. There was no great revelation, just the inner resolution that it was time to move on—now.

"I informed my boss the next day," he says. "He claimed he didn't understand what I was talking about. He said he was sorry to lose me, but I really didn't believe him. He could care less whether I lived or died. I walked out the door that day scared as could be, but at peace with my decision."

This story describes an encounter with God, yet the discovery hardly seems dramatic or noteworthy. It reads more like a thoughtful life transition than a mind-altering visitation of

God's power and might. Yet even in all its ordinariness, we can identify several components of this encounter and show how they lead to a deeper relationship with God.

A New Clarity

A clarity comes when we involve God in our decision making. This can take place through a quiet meeting with God in prayer, the scriptures or some richly reflective activity. Some spiritual sojourners simply describe a clarity that takes shape in the middle of a crisis. Others speak of a long-term wrestling bout with the powers of darkness before they see the light. In all, the clarity enlightens them about a specific direction for their lives. In ancient monastic terms, this is a divine lesson, a *Lectio Divina*.

What is so interesting is that the deep connection with God and the development of a new self evolve together. Michael Casey suggests that persons can often face the unknown within themselves because they find a grounding in God. This allows them to take new risks. "Self-knowledge and Godknowledge," he suggests, "go hand in hand."[7]

Ultimately, all growth is a reflection of God's creative action, yet the process of a deepening self matures decision by decision, effort by effort.

A Sense of Rightness

Over time, the struggle for clarity opens up into a second level: an intuitive awareness that the decisions, directions and hunger to know God more deeply are *right for me*. An awareness settles in that my true home is found in the familiar ground of love.

A friend of ours once summarized the deepening confirmation of the rightness of his choices as we celebrated a private liturgy.

"I have been in monastic life for fifty years," he said, "and I'm too old to change now, nor would I really want to. I do have to admit that I have gone through years of uncertainty about the inner workings of the monastic community. It is a lot easier than it was in 1948, but the call is still a difficult one."

"Nevertheless," he affirmed with a clear conviction, "I live in the growing presence of a loving God, who continues to invite me into the deeper regions of love. I think about the words of the psalmist, 'taste and see the goodness of the Lord.' Sometimes all my senses are involved; sometimes it's pretty dark and vague, but all in all, the love of God sustains me and gives me life."

Hunger: The Language of a Spirituality

"Like the deer that yearns for running streams, so my soul is longing for you, my God."

This opening line of Psalm 42 articulates the language of every genuine spirituality: Hunger drives and forms it. Even a mature spirituality does not adequately satisfy the longings of the human heart. The hunger simply becomes more refined as a spirituality deepens.

A number of years ago, we attended the first of the International Thomas Merton Society conferences, hosted by Bellarmine College in Louisville, Kentucky. The location certainly seemed appropriate, for the college is the home of the Thomas Merton archives. Here, original texts, letters, journals and documents from the Merton era are preserved, open to scholars in their continued study of his works.

On Sunday, the conference group was invited to the Trappist monastery at Gethsemani, Merton's home for twenty-seven years, for a liturgy, picnic and poetry reading at Merton's hermitage.

As we drove the highway between Louisville and Bardstown, the early morning sun warmed the temperature to the low seventies. A phalanx of brilliant red and yellow flowers guided us southward. With years of reflection on Merton's works behind us, we recounted how much this trip to Gethsemani felt like a homecoming, even though we had never before seen the place. Anticipation of what awaited us opened the terrain into a rich landscape of love.

We arrived at the abbey church in plenty of time to join the Sunday liturgy. It came alive with incense, psalmody, modern song and a fine talk by Flavian Burns, Abbot of Gethsemani during the last chapter of Merton's life. The spirit of Merton was as contagious as the smells of springtime.

The liturgy finished, the two of us walked freely about the abbey church, speaking in whispers about the experience, the place and the man who still wielded such a powerful influence over us. An older monk then approached us, caught our smiles, then returned his own.

"Oh, hello," he said, "are you two friends of Father Louis?"

We both paused and laughed, tickled by the use of Thomas Merton's monastic name to invite us into dialogue.

"As a matter of fact, we are," P. J. answers.

"I was a novice under Father Louis," the old monk announced, clearly identifying himself with that proud fraternity who learned the principles of the monastic life under its master. We stood listening to him, not sure how to respond to this chance encounter.

"I had a dream about Father Louis last night," he continued. "I dreamed I was back in class, enjoying every moment of what he was telling us. In my dream, he came to me as a visitor from heaven, to reassure me that he is very happy. He told me not to worry about the small things in life, as it so quickly passes. God will bring my life to fullness like he did his, in God's own time."

The encounter was a gentle one; the old monk shared himself so openly. He adopted us into his fraternity of love as we affirmed our common ground with him.

"Tell us," P. J. asked, "what do you remember most about Merton's classes on spirituality?"

The monk paused.

"Hunger," he answered, "the spiritual life is a life of hunger. We hunger so for God, and as we progress into the life of God we do find peace, yet the hunger gets more intense. Father Louis was always telling us we learn more from the hunger than we do from the theologians. I have never forgotten that."

The Hunger for the Hidden Ground of Love

As we reaffirmed in our own little awakening that day at Gethsemani, God's reality becomes the ground of our life a little at a time. God uses ordinary events to engage us in extraordinary ways.

God gently opens the ground of love that exists beneath us, in us, all around us, and we begin to know God in every event, each experience. God slowly awakens all our responses, all our desires, then focuses them on the one reality that underlies all other realities: God's own person.

The hunger for God manifests itself in uncountable ways. It

is a longing for the transcendent. It is an ache that will not go away. It drives us to explore the deeper implications of life. It is often felt as an irrepressible urge to pray. It is generally more of a restlessness than a clarity. It can even seem like a burden at times, especially when the hunger intensifies through unexpected darkness or unwanted suffering. Yet the very things that seem so burdensome can become the richest of God's gifts.

Michael Casey describes this powerful drive to discover God as a *discontent*,[8] and he sees it as a power that underlies the quest for all spirituality. This basic energy drives us to search for answers to our deepest longings.

The more we address that subtle, sure calling of deep hunger within, the more God responds, as God slowly seduces us to enter into a dynamic relationship with God and with one another.

In brief, the hunger is the drive that invites us to enter into the mystery of love. Its ground lies in dormant anticipation of our arrival, beckoning us to explore it through the hunger that refuses to let go.

The Central Place of Love

It is love that invites us to break out of the narrow confines of our lives and explore new possibilities for our restless spirits. It is love that invites us to look for a destiny that lies just beyond our capacity to define it. Love invites us to open ourselves to another and to journey together into a rich and satisfying union.

The evangelist John states it very simply: "God is love and anyone who lives in love lives in God, and God lives in him" (1 Jn **4:16**).

William Shannon, theologian, spiritual writer and internationally recognized Merton scholar, believes the search for love ends in union with God as the very ground of love. All of life becomes an expression of this grounding. The development of an identity, an appreciation of our own uniqueness and the trustworthy context for relating to others, all come to fullness in this fertile ground of love.[9]

As we hear consistently from the couples with whom we work, their grounding in God is the deepest source of their life and love. It changes the quality of their marriage. As they become aware of God as unconditional love, they relate in a more compassionate mode. Their marriage becomes the most concrete expression of the love of God.

Marital Spirituality Is a Shared Spirituality

We come back, now, to the second half of our phrase, *marital spirituality*. Everything we have written thus far about the nature of spirituality applies in a unique way to marital spirituality. It is reflective, aimed at the exploration of profound truths and grounded in love. It seeks to discover a true self. Yet marital spirituality has a texture and a uniqueness all its own. It develops through a consistent and serious *sharing of lives*.

In an individual spirituality, the interior life of the person may never be known by anyone else, and it makes little difference. In marital spirituality, however, the sharing of interiority is not a luxury; it forms the very substance of the spirituality itself. The experience is different for every couple.

We have made an effort to live a vital spirituality in our marriage of twenty-four years, so we know how rich the sharing can be. The reading of the scriptures each day *(Lectio Divina)* keeps us grounded in an awareness that God enlivens our love in gentle ways.

We also work together every day, dealing with the complex

problems of living on behalf of our clients. If we grow uncertain about direction, we reflect back on the awareness cultivated in our early morning prayer time.

Lectio Divina has taught us that marital intimacy is not an end in itself, grounded in an obsessive enterprise to feel good under all circumstances. It is an opening up of love that becomes more life-giving as it matures.

Should we grow uncertain about what the demands of life entail, we bring one another back to the deeper truths of our existence. These redirections are at times gentle, at other times confrontational.

We support and love one another in the shared awareness that God is with us in every effort of our life. We know God as the deepening ground of our love. We call upon this ground to firm up as we move, day by day, through the challenges of a shared life. It sustains us as we live out the agenda of our healing ministry.

At the end of the day, we measure our efforts to love by comparing them to the gospel ideal. If we fall short, we prompt one another to try harder. If we have grown, we affirm our hard efforts. In all, we bring our awareness full circle to where we began the day: grounded in the hunger that drives us to enter ever more deeply into the hidden ground of love.

This kind of sharing challenges us to love ever more honestly. The continued dynamic of sharing invites us never to allow our individual efforts to flag and weaken.

We also offer workshops to married couples on the many dimensions of married spirituality. This invites us to dialogue with couples as they make a serious effort to pursue their desires for a rich marriage. Allow us to share some of their comments about how God touches their lives. Each one of these statements confirms a strong connection between a sound spirituality and deep sharing:

"Marital spirituality reminds us of how loving God is in our lives."

"It brings us back consistently to our own truths."

"It invites us to bring out the best in one another, because we know that this is what God wants."

"Marital spirituality leads to more and more discovery—facing the awesome realities of what a marriage is."

"It helps us find meaning in the thousand little events of our life. Somehow, we find that these little events matter to God."

"It invites us to share the deepest part of our selves and to feel at home there."

"Marital spirituality helps me to cope with the thousands of little irritants that are part of marriage and not to let them overwhelm me."

Interpersonal Process Is Important as Well

Verbal sharing is one way to enter into the richness of a marital spirituality. Not every deep experience in marriage, however, can be contained in words. The purity of this example speaks to the power of presence, attentiveness and compassion.

"I awoke one night in a cold sweat," he begins. "My wife is sleeping peacefully beside me, knowing nothing about my inner turmoil. I become acutely aware of how, even in the best of loves, so many things contaminate it.

"I am a worrier from the word go," he continues. "I am as guilty as most middle-class people of focusing everything on money and equating money with security. Now my imagination starts to run away with me; I can feel my responses quickening.

"I begin to become fearful of the fact that I am at the age where corporate America no longer needs me, because I am in my late forties and overspecialized.

"What if I lose my job? I ask. How is my new district manager going to react to my honesty about the way I see things? I begin to sweat more; I feel an overwhelming anxiety rush over me.

"I'm no longer a young person," he continues. "I have only so many resources saved for emergencies, perhaps enough to live for six months. The anxiety is beginning to get to me. Then my wife stirs, wakes up, perhaps sensing my fears. She asks me if I'd like to talk. We do so, and I share my fears. She embraces me and tells me not to worry, that she is convinced of God's loyalty to us. She then falls asleep in my arms.

"I'm not sure what happened," he continues. "It might be the tenderness she showed me. She can calm me with the simplest statement. She also confronts my craziness."

God speaks to married couples through the penetrating experience of a shared love, yet the richest language of love is often a warm embrace, a spontaneous assurance, or a gesture of solidarity. God becomes visible and real as they learn to understand the subtle language of love.

Sexuality Is Central

Married love is profoundly sexual, since God creates the sexes out of the fathomless mystery of God's own love. God creates us men and women, and the riches of a marital spirituality blossom within the creative expressiveness of a mature sexuality.

Evelyn and James Whitehead, a husband and wife team of social scientist and theologian, assert correctly that sexuality lies at the core of every marriage. Thus, exchanges of affection, a sharing of sexual selves, the joy and the frustrations of learning to become good lovers are all expressions of a developing marital spirituality.[10]

Our work carries us into the intimate center of marriage. At the center of every good marriage is a tender and loving sense of sexuality. Couples vary immensely in their expressiveness of this sexuality, but they are clear concerning one thing: they learn a great deal about their own value and the value of their spouse as they become more sexual.

Listen to the dialogue of this couple as they explain the evolution of their marital sexuality and how it has brought them into a deeper understanding of their experience of love.

"At first it was all fever and intensity," he says. "The passion was so strong, we tried to devour each other."

"This is true," she laughs; "we couldn't get enough of one another."

"About the tenth year of our marriage, we hit a decline. I got real dysfunctional."

"It was difficult for both of us," she asserts. "I lost interest."

"So we got some help, and I learned a lot about the ways that women deal with their sexuality. She is not like me: She cannot separate her sexual response from honest talk. I had expected her to be loving and tender even when I was intense and abrasive."

"I couldn't do that," she says. "He expected me to be responsive while he never shared anything of himself or what I meant to him. I don't understand how men can be so detached—so physical."

"The best part of the learning is how deeply we each feel,

and we learned to share more from the soul—ya know, the inner self."

"It is beautiful," she affirms. "My sexual desires began to come back to life because I could finally feel something for him."

"I, in turn," he states, "realized I could feel more. It took me several months to begin to understand that my dysfunction was tied to my angry feelings. It was a way that my body was telling her, 'No deal: no sex, no talk.'"

"We are coming back to life," she asserts, a little tearfully.

"In ways that are new to me," he laughs.

"Our sexuality is now alive and well and we are discovering a beauty in the joys of simple touch and sharing that have recharged our sexual desires."

Sam Keen, modern philosopher and writer, reflects at length about the close connection between sexual fulfillment and becoming whole. He is candidly honest about his own experiences and how his earlier life taught him so much about sexuality.

At the center of any vital sexuality in marriage, he believes, are a number of other qualities that, developed to a fine edge, offer depth and meaning to the sexual experience. He suggests paying attention to a partner, listening, expressing compassion and sharing a deep sensuality.[11]

We often suggest to our couples a process of slowing down, learning to be present to one another, seeing a pleasurable and sensitive sexual interlude as sacramental. By affirming this kind of sensual sacramentality, we suggest that the expression of love to one another is a concretization of the hidden mystery of Love who is God. In this way, a lived sexuality opens up a profound experience of God's love.

The God Who Waits for Us

Marital spirituality can be defined, then, as *a shared quest for the hidden ground of love*. This definition is a general one, yet it tells us a great deal about the energy, source, hunger and desire implied in the quest to live a rich life of love. It leaves open the question of differences among couples, for there are innumerable ways that couples construct the practical dimensions of marital spirituality.

How they translate their experience of love into a lived reality depends on their vision, their hopes, their capacity to problem-solve, their comfort with intimacy and their ability to maintain their individuality.

As a couple progresses toward the source of Love who is God, they find an array of both joys and surprises. The invitation to savor the challenge of love is both gratifying and anxiety provoking.

The progression into a deeper love fills a person with the joy of fulfillment. It invites the best from a spouse, engaging heart and soul in ways that no other human experience can touch. Only a genuine love brings about the final resolution of human restlessness.

Yet the same joining invites intense anxiety, because love calls forth a range of responses most couples would just as soon forget. This is a journey that promises more than simply feeling good, because to know the landscape is to be asked to let go of the distortions that do not allow love to mature. This can be a painful and difficult matter, but the God who creates the hunger also satisfies it.

Marriage, like no other human endeavor, invites us into the hidden realm of love. The entry into this ground is really nothing more than an effort to make explicit what many couples know intuitively: that an entry into love yields a rich harvest because it is the dwelling place of the Sacred.

They know that God dwells in this place. God has pitched his tent in their backyards or in their hearts and souls, and lives there with them. God is there all the time, inviting the couple to understand all that this reality promises. They spend the rest of their lives making this event real for one another.

Chapter 2: Into the Hidden Ground of Love

The notion of God as the hidden ground of love is certainly not a new idea, nor are we the first to explore the relationship between God and interpersonal process. The First Letter of John reminds us very simply:

> ...let us love one another since love comes from God and everyone who loves is begotten by God and knows God. Anyone who fails to love can never have known God, because God is love.
>
> (1 Jn 4:7)

In seeking a fresh expression for how the mystery of love gives form and substance to marital spirituality, we find ourselves inevitably returning to a stream of tradition that seeks God as the first source and final end of all love. One branch of the stream flows from the western monastic tradition, where total transformation in love is both the foundation and the ideal of the Christian life. We draw freely from this tradition, for it holds out to us a treasury of wisdom open to anyone, whether married or single.

As the old saying goes, "marriages are made of something old and something new." By centering our reflections on something old—the origins of love, its powerful dynamic and its end in God—we identify our explorations with a rich tradition.

By examining the centrality of love in contemporary marital spirituality, we discover something new. Yet whether old or new, these explorations of love still hold in common the genuine hunger for God, and this hunger seems to be an authentic human endeavor.

Sam Keen asserts, for example, that the gospel of the possibility of love, "seems to be built into human nature."[12] He suggests that to look at love in this transcendent way is an embarrassment to our modern minds.

We find, however, little evidence of embarrassment among those couples with whom we dialogue, for one indisputable fact emerges: They long to find something lasting and fulfilling in their efforts to love. This longing drives them to explore the depths of love, and their exploration brings them to a discovery of an unbreakable connection with God.

Herbert Benson, M.D., course director of Harvard's Spirituality and Healing in Medicine program, is another contemporary voice that speaks to the question of how solidly we are grounded in God. He begins his exploration with an awakening that began with his father's untimely death with rheumatic heart disease.

His thirty-year quest to find the eternal truths about the human experience brought him to a conviction that our bodies are actually wired to benefit not only from exercising our muscles, but from exercising more lasting matters: beliefs, values, thoughts and feelings.[13]

Thirty years later, his research, experience, discussion and teaching lead him to assert that human beings are in a profound, physical way "wired for God." More than any other effort, prayer accesses this connection.

Our brains are so wired, he contends, that we will not be incapacitated by the acknowledgment and dread of death, but they will point us toward "a better, nobler meaning to life."[14]

Although Benson addresses the question of healing rather than the place of love in the human endeavor, we offer a logical connection between the old and the new by suggesting a simple syllogism:

The human person is wired for God.
God is love.
Therefore, the human person is wired for love.

Looking for Deeper Ground

In our efforts to articulate a deep marital spirituality, we turn toward the monastic spirit as described by Thomas Merton. We turn to him because he helps us give form and definition to the dimensions of love that are not immediately evident in the surface interactions of marriage.

We also look at his writings because he blends old and new, the monastic spirit of solitude and a deep hunger for personal love. He blends the wisdom of the East and the intellectual acumen of the West in a fascinating personal journey that carried him into the depths of divine love. He is singularly prominent among spiritual authors in his efforts to express the ultimately inexpressible: God as love, the ground of our being.

Merton was a gifted monk who reflected for most of his adult years on the mystery of God's love, then wrote at length about it. Early in his monastic journey he focused on a narrow view of the reflective life, separating himself from the world in a 1940s style of Catholicism. As his writing matured, especially through the 1960s, he corresponded with admirers from all over the world.

This correspondence was responsible for a significant broadening of his ideas, for he dialogued with political figures, literary types, religious leaders and philosophers from diverse backgrounds. He was influential in their lives, as they were in his. Consequently, his later writings reflect a view of the Sacred that speaks to those who seriously explore the place of the transcendent God in all of life. In today's terms, we can say that he possessed a global consciousness.

As his whole life suggested, the real journey in life is interior. His writings chart the life of the inner spirit. He examined a significant number of themes that speak to the deep action of love at work in the human heart.[15]

In the depths of love, a transformation takes place. He speaks of it often as a transformation of the self. By that he means not only a change in a person's emotions, attitudes or perceptions, but a transformation of the hidden inner self where the connection with God forms the very ground of personal existence.

Merton does not take issue with the changes of feelings, the redirecting of energy or the expansiveness that falling in love fosters. These are primarily psychological and emotional matters. He knows enough about the human qualities of love in his own life to speak authoritatively to the real changes that a powerful love experience brings with it. He describes these matters at great length in his personal journals.

He was more interested in the largely invisible yet dramatically real transformation of the deeper self that takes place through an encounter with God. He spent a lifetime of serious and sometimes anguishing reflection on his own existence and explored at length how the ground of love opens out into an intimate relationship with God.

This ground influences more than the psychological or the emotional dimensions of life; this is the ground of existence. This is the realm of what Merton called the *true self*. Like a butterfly emerging from its winter cocoon, the layers of the self come to life. As anyone who has fallen deeply in love can attest, a new world breaks through our consciousness. Our vision becomes expansive. We stand in the presence of hidden majesty.[16]

This awakening sensitivity to the mystery of our existence changes not only our selves, it remakes the ways we relate to God. God is not something "out there," but God resides in the deepest interior dimension of our life: the true self. The ground of love, which is God, literally forms the mystery of our existence.

But What about Marriage?

So just what is the hidden ground of love in a marital spirituality? Can it be easily defined? Is it a complex psychological process in which a person finds a rich and rewarding love? Is it an emotional/sexual awakening that leads to inner harmony?

Or is it a mystery so profound that we can speak only tentatively of the deeper realms of human existence, hardwired as we are by our Creator to know the full implications of the mystery of love only in death?

We suggest an answer that is really no answer at all: The hidden ground of love contains elements of all of the above. It is both a psychological (perceptions, feelings, attitudes) and an ontological reality (God as ground of our being).

42

Love forms the deepest roots of who we are. The emergence of love calls forth a powerful emotional experience and invites the best from our reservoir of collected awarenesses and learned responses. It invites us to climb to the heights of the human experience, to write poetry and to celebrate the joy of being human.

Yet there is more to love than the impassioned responses of a lover. It is expansive; it fosters a unity with all reality. Love forms the connection between our human experience and divine love.

For Christians, the hidden ground of love is, at its deepest reality, the person of God. For it is God who breathes into us the breath of life and sustains us. It is God who breathes life into our marriages, who forms the deepest foundation for opening up to one another. The notion of the hidden ground of love, then, includes several diverse dimensions, yet they all speak of the joys and the challenges of love.

A year before Merton died, he tried to capture a vision of these dimensions in a letter to a friend. Because his task is dauntless, his vision is sweeping. For his critics, his vision is too grandiose to be useful, but we suggest it is full of wisdom.

"...call it Being," he writes, "...call it Atman, call it Pneuma... or Silence."[17]

In this simple phrase, he suggests that love transcends even our capacity to define it. No one word captures its essence. No one system of belief adequately expresses all that love is.

Understanding what love is and how it forms the ground of our being is more a matter of "being attentive" or "learning to listen" to the echoes of love all around us. It brings about a genuine happiness that cannot be adequately explained. Merton describes this happiness as "being at one with everything in that hidden ground of love for which there are no explanations."[18]

To make an effort to explore and expand the notions Merton hints at, allow us to reflect on his thoughts in a piece-meal fashion. By doing so, we will make an effort to use Merton's own vocabulary to launch an exploration of the deeper dimensions of marital spirituality.

"...call it Being...."

Working with marriages remains rewarding work, even after twenty-three years. For the most part, our work is aimed at realigning the entangled interaction of couples. We help them find relief from a variety of dysfunctions that haunt them: conflicted communication, anger over small injustices, disappointment over unfulfilled expectations and the inability to resolve conflicts.

For most couples, the work proceeds uneventfully. They learn to approach one another more openly, then find that healing flows from this repositioning. With confidence in their new skills, they generally move into a renewed phase of their marriage. In brief, they enjoy a more satisfactory relationship and a more fulfilling love.

This renewal generally brings with it less conflict, but it often invites a couple to explore the deeper dimensions of a shared life. Energy once spent on hard problem solving can now be invested in creating a vision for their marriage. In general, they begin to discover a spirituality, and they look to us to help them establish it.

"We're still not satisfied, even after all our talk," a wife states. "There is still something missing for us, and we can't get ahold of it."

"What about a spirituality?" we ask. "We know that interaction forms the day-to-day stuff of relating, but a deeper bond, and certainly a meaning to life, flows out of a spirituality."

"But we have never pursued anything like that," her husband says. "We both grew up Catholic, but drifted away from it during our college years. It just does not speak to us about anything other than guilt."

"That is only one pathway," we suggest. "Perhaps some of what was good about it will come back, but you don't begin a spirituality by reclaiming something essentially negative for you. Spirituality is an opening up, an effort to find a deeper reality for your lives. If you have a hunger for it, you need only try to relate to the hunger. It will lead you to an opening."

This conversation, as simple as it seems, encouraged this couple to begin to explore a spirituality after ten years of marriage. The first option they tested was a marriage renewal program at a local church.

The workshop stimulated them to continue to pursue a spirituality more seriously and, five years later, they have developed one that speaks to their needs. It is simple in its content: they break away four times a year to dialogue about life, love and their future.

This offers them a predictable renewal time. Sometimes they take advantage of structured growth experiences in their community, sometimes not. They love to read, and structure growth around a capacity to encourage one another to "stretch a little" with fresh ideas.

When asked to describe what they mean now by their spirituality, they speak in these terms:

"We have depth now we never had before," she says. "I feel good about us. Love is so different. We are more patient and tolerant. We have discovered a deeper level of love that we can tap into when we need it."

"It is different, now," he agrees. "We are not as adrift as we once were, or so demanding in our relationship. We have roots we can trust."

We suggest that this couple's experience of discovery touches on several meanings of Merton's word, *being*. This notion of being is a practical one, because it relates to a more open interpersonal climate. Hence, they enjoy a better relationship. This enhances their feelings of wholeness both within themselves and within the relationship.

They intuitively know that they are anchored in a more reliable foundation for love even if they cannot define it clearly. They are more secure in their interaction. In brief, they enjoy a state of well-being. In this context, the notion of *being* relates to a psychological and emotional state of creative living.

This couple's efforts to develop their love more honestly will lead them into the deeper ground of love that awaits them. That shift not only enhances their sensitivity in a psychological and emotional fashion, it will touch a deeper sense of *being:* their very existence. Being at this level in a marriage reflects a shared awareness of a destiny grounded in God as pure Love. Sharing around this ultimate reality confirms their destiny.

"...call it Atman...."

One Saturday afternoon finds the two of us in the Nelson Gallery in Kansas City. Its massive building and manicured gardens shelter one of the finest oriental art collections in the nation. The entire complex offers a welcome refuge from the commercial madness that governs life just several blocks away.

At 2:17, we walk into a massive oriental display room and

face an imposing wall, its sandstone surface carved with an elaborate collection of Hindu deities. The wall overwhelms us, extending upward a full three stories and spanning the eighty-foot width of the room.

The identifier card notes this is an ancient temple wall, its origins in China, eighth century B.C.E. The male deities, collection of goddesses and congealed images of the divine glare down at us. They stir mixed emotions, like entering a room full of extended family members, some on good terms, some not.

The powerful assembly of heavenly personalities stretches from floor to ceiling, overshadowing our small presence. We simply stand staring, open-mouthed and inert, looking for a resolution of the tension.

The room is markedly quiet. It contrasts dramatically with the noisy corridors of the gallery, filled with visiting children from area schools.

A separate figure, a statue, suddenly and forcefully captures our awareness, tearing us away from our fixation on the stone edifice. She gazes down at us in a penetrating look from eight feet above our heads. We marvel at the sheer beauty of this statue: smooth polished stone, like fine alabaster. The statue is identified as *Quan Yin*, the Hindu goddess of compassion.

We are two strangers immersed in a Hindu world that essentially overpowers us. This is the realm of Brahman, the underlying unity of all things. Hinduism, like all the eastern religions, turns its face toward the contemplation of oneness.

The busyness of the Hindu deities is the realm of Atman: a specific embodiment in space and time of Brahman. Each deity takes on a specific quality contained in the One. The aura of compassion, embodied so powerfully by *Quan Yin*, overshadows our small presence and pulls at us to open up into the oneness of the compassionate experience.

The statue also dates to the eighth century B.C.E. and originally guarded the harbor of a Chinese fishing village. The name, *Quan Yin,* is literally translated as "She Who hearkens to the cries of the world."

Dark narrow eyes that intensify a sensual feeling identify her in the Hindu belief system as the embodiment of compassion. She carries her sensuality with grace and composure. We begin to feel secure in her presence, even though this is our first encounter with *Quan Yin.* Her presence involves us at an emotional level, evaporating our tensions.

We invite our minds to settle in and absorb the quiet. We deepen our feeling for this powerful work of art. We feel ourselves forcefully pulled out of the constraints of body, time and place, and enter into sacred space. There is no resisting the pull, for even within its abruptness, it maintains the unique feel and sustaining tenderness of compassionate energy.

The space intensifies in its power and immensity. We feel it, absorb it, allow it to touch the depths of our separate beings. We are not strangers to the energy of compassion, so we allow ourselves to dwell in her space. It is familiar territory, already consecrated through our encounters with the compassionate God of Christianity. Even though the personality of *Quan Yin* is unfamiliar to us, her presence opens up an experience of the feminine quality of compassion, too often missing in our masculine images of God.

Our sacred time in this realm brings with it no duality, no competition between the Christian God of compassion and a great mix of Hindu deities. All is one for a time, embraced in a compassionate womb that removes the crusty barriers of history, gender and competition.

We already know our God as compassion, and *Quan Yin* brings with her a cosmic connection: The engaging space we feel as the feminine quality of compassionate love is expanded and deepened into an immersion in God. All is one; all is well.

As in all deeply engaging experiences, we long to remain in this sea of compassion and oneness, but we cannot. The pressures of life plant us solidly back on our feet, then send us out to the clamor of commercial life. We leave the space behind, but it fills us. It gives texture and vitality to our relationship with every person we encounter for several weeks.

Ancient devotion to *Quan Yin* tells us that it is compassion that unifies reality. It is the feminine quality of compassion that undergirds the transitory conditions of life and gives them form. The feminine is the ground of a rich interplay between materiality and spiritual energy.

Merton's reference to "Atman" seems real at this captivating moment, for we are immersed in the oneness of all being. Atman is the gateway. A global expansiveness still remains part of our consciousness, inviting us to be deeply respectful of the love we carry for one another. It is very sacred; it is part of the One. We gain a taste of the powerful waves of happiness that Merton describes as the reward for entering into the oneness of creation.

"...call it Pneuma...or Silence...."

We stand in front of forty-five married couples on a sharply cold Friday evening in January. It is snowing lightly outside. The woods are filling up with light powder, but inside the lodgelike convention center, an oak fire burns brightly in the large stone fireplace, bathing the room with warmth. For the next two hours, we face a formidable task: Take this diverse group of couples and open them up to a serious reflection on what their marriages can mean. They come because they share an interest in developing a marital spirituality.

Most of them have small children at home, yet they are willing to take a precious Friday evening and Saturday to renew their marriages. We know little about their histories, so we fall back on our "one-third" rule of personal survival: One-third of them are probably living in healthy marriages already, one-third are a mix of functionality and dysfunction, and one-third are in serious trouble.

This easy division of reality allows us to move through our presentations with limited expectations. We know that some couples use a conference of this type as a last resort to resolve their stubborn problems. Their expectations for an eleventh-hour miracle are high. Nevertheless, we begin our work with enthusiasm.

"There is no better place to begin a reflection on the nature of marital spirituality," P. J. begins, "than with the book of Genesis."

The reflection on *Ruah Yahweh* (the breath of God image, taken from the Old Testament book of Genesis) begins. As it is read slowly and with a little emphasis, the Genesis creation account begins to come to life.

P. J. continues: "God is present in the story as a powerful wind, a creative spirit who longs to bring a fullness to the world...so God takes mud and like a potter forms this *adamah,* this mud thing, then breathes into the nostrils of this thing and it became a living person....We exist as human beings because God breathes into us the breath of life."

Like the first subtle stirring of life on earth, they get it. The couples move inward and begin to reflect on the greatest of gifts: being itself—human existence—and its connection to marriage.

"Look at Genesis not as history, but as present moment," P. J. continues. "God is breathing into you the breath of life as you face God now. Your very breathing is a response to God, an act of gratitude, and the first prayer begins as you become aware of the significance of your breathing. Prayer is a conscious effort to breathe in this great mystery and to absorb the presence of God into your bones and flesh."

Claudette picks up the theme: "God gives us life and presents us to one another, woman and man, with all our likenesses and our differences. God invites us to come to life and to express this life by loving one another. The Genesis story is woven together into a fine fabric: The first gifts are life and love. They are two facets of God's creative expression and our acceptance of them in gratitude opens us up to the presence of God."

The tension in the room lessens a bit, so we play with words and wade into the stream of tradition that connects the old and the new, *Ruah* and *Pneuma*, since both words flow from a common origin.

Merton borrowed the word *Pneuma* from the New Testament Greek, because it, too, describes the breath of God, Who breathes life into the new community. In the Gospels, Jesus breathes on his disciples and fills them with the Holy Spirit. They therefore breathe with the power of God to heal, to forgive sins, to spread the kingdom of heaven.

The Holy Spirit came on Pentecost as a roaring wind—the breath of God. It brings a dramatic change to the early church community: It is transformed from a fearful sect to a dynamic gathering of believers who change the face of the earth.

Now our instruction focuses on some new ways to go about praying, and it begins to make sense to the couples. We invite them to slow down, to be still and know that God is

God by focusing on their breathing. This exercise begins to open them to the riches God desires to give them. We invite them into intimacy with God and with one another. The moment of creation is *now*.

The couples begin to understand that they share the gifts of life and marriage simply because they are chosen by God. Their slowing down, breathing together, allows them to enter into the domain of God's love for which they hunger.

It is very quiet. The fire burns brightly. Smells of burning oak coax them to let go. A new awareness is unfolding, as gentle as soft breathing, as immediate as a heartbeat. God is the source of all reality: the ground of being. Silence unites us to the splendor of creation.

"Pay attention to your breathing," Claudette coaches, weighing her words almost a syllable at a time. "Slow down. Catch your breath. Genesis is now, for God creates us continually, inviting us to explore the very origins of our consciousness by living and moving in love."

Merton speaks of *Pneuma*, "breath," as our connection with the ground of love. Under the quiet spell of the woods, the Genesis story and a warm fire, some of the couples hold hands as they center themselves. The whole group finds a peaceful home in the quiet atmosphere of love and breathes in its reality. They know this is where they belong.

As Merton reminds us, "...the simple fact of being attentive, by learning to listen...we find ourselves engulfed in such happiness that it cannot be explained."[19]

We have already hinted at the rewards for simply being, so now let us say a few things about attentiveness and listening, and how they enrich a marital spirituality.

"...being attentive...."

Of all the qualities necessary to move inward, quiet time is the most difficult state for married couples to achieve. The mere mention of its importance can bring about a negative reaction, for couples are quick to point out that they are incessantly busy with the demands of family life.

Yet, we insist there is always a way to find some quiet time in any marriage. We affirm that an attentiveness to one another is so critical that a marriage will die without it.

Sam Keen notes that attentiveness is the first gift we make in the name of love. He contrasts it to the lethal habit of taking someone for granted.[20] Attentiveness is critical to the life of a relationship, calling forth from spouses a kind of self-denial. It places the other in a primary position.

"What," we ask our couples, "could be so pressing that there is no time to be present to one another? How much time does it take to stay bonded? Why are other matters always so pressing that we ignore the person we supposedly love the most?"

We offer them a simple axiom: "Those couples who want to be present to one another will always find a few minutes to be together; those who flee the demands of intimacy will always find something more important."

The practicality of attentiveness might mean getting up earlier in the morning in order to spend quality time together as husband and wife, not as overly stressed parents.

Some couples maintain the tradition of a special night out for themselves, free of the obligations that can deaden a marriage.

Attentiveness can even foster a transition to a simpler form of prayer. A couple might simply sit together in prayerful silence, holding on to an awareness of God's love for them. Silence of this kind becomes a deep act of sharing.

"...by learning to listen...."

Marriage calls couples to enter ever more earnestly into a dialogue of love with one another. This implies *listening,* and we call this art "attentiveness in action." We invite couples to hear one another's feelings, experiences, most urgent longings, hardest challenges, deepest hurts, and dreams of a future. Listening, then, reflects a genuine compassion (a sensitive identification with a spouse in order to know him or her in depth).

"We were burnt out," confesses Tina, as she explores her family relationships after ten years of marriage.

"The stresses in my extended family have been incredible. One of my family always surfaces when I need them the least; then they expect me to solve their problems. My brother still won't speak to me because I refused to bankroll him for a new house. Anyway, my husband and I were at one another's throats. We couldn't talk about anything without conflict."

"She's not kidding," George adds, shaking his head as he confirms her observations. "We were after one another constantly. We blamed one another for everything that went wrong. We finally decided to spend some of our savings to find some personal space instead of bailing out her brother."

"We didn't even let my family know where we were," Tina adds. "In less than twenty-four hours, we were drinking mai tais and walking the seashore on Aruba. We listened to one another for the first time in years."

Catching Our Breath

An entry into the deeper realm of love can begin with a simple exercise in breathing. We often refer to this exercise in centering as "catching our breath." It reconstructs a link with the source of our being, who revitalizes us as we breathe in the breath of God *(Ruah Yahweh)*. It is a reflection of the New Testament *Pneuma:* God breathing into us the gift of life. We invite you and your partner to explore a richer ground of love through the following exercise.

Place yourselves in a family room, secluded space or favorite hideout where no one knows you dwell, and be alone with one another for thirty minutes. If you have children, make sure they are gone or quiet, and that you will not be disturbed by them. Take the phone off the hook.

Sit quietly in one another's presence. Foster this quiet inner space by closing your eyes and breathing slowly, while quietly saying a phrase to yourself: "Pause a while and know that I am God" (Ps 46:10 JB). Remember, God gives you breath as an expression of God's love, so breathe in the reality of God's love slowly and let it center you.

As you begin to quiet down, you may find a tendency to get distracted as your mind returns to the pressing matters of the day. You may find yourself feeling guilty, getting uncomfortable with the process or wishing you were elsewhere.

The best way to deal with these distractions is not to deal with them at all, because the harder you work to override them, the more stubborn they become. Return to the slow repetition of your quieting phrase and enjoy the evolving peacefulness. "Pause awhile and know that I am God" invites you to change the focus of your life to an inward peace, where God dwells.

After ten minutes of quieting down by catching your breath in this manner, we invite you to move toward an infusion of new energy by turning to the scriptures. We offer a *Lectio Divina*, taken from one of our couple workshops.

Lectio Divina:
The Hidden Treasure

In the Gospel of Matthew (13:44), Jesus speaks of the mysterious kingdom of heaven. The Gospel presents information in stories and parables for a good reason, for we cannot speak definitively about the inner life of God; this belongs only to God. Nor can we easily construct clear and certain knowledge of God, for God remains the Unknowable One. We can only approach the Sacred respectfully and tentatively, allowing the stories and parables to light the way.

Take the next ten minutes and read to one another thoughtfully and deliberately, taking time to slow down your pace to help you savor the words of the text. Read it several times in a thoughtful fashion, then pause, while you each reflect on its meaning. The brief text could yield a different meaning each time that you read it.

> "The kingdom of heaven is like treasure hidden in a field which someone has found; he hides it again, goes off happy, sells everything he owns and buys the field."
>
> (Mt 13:44)

As you can see, the parable is a brief one, and in the course of ten minutes it can be repeated several times. Let the silence between the readings speak to you as you turn over the meaning of the text in your mind.

You can think of these actions of respectful repetition and personal absorption as an infusion of new energy for your lives. The energy flows directly from the inner life of God. Slow down your pace even more and breathe in the new life. Let the atmosphere of silent reflection speak to you about how significant this energy is for you at this moment.

At a deeper level, the person of Jesus is entering the quiet sanctuary of your marriage, speaking directly to you about the dignity of your love. Allow Jesus to become the teacher about the value of your life, your marriage, your destiny.

From our perspective, the entirety of the text speaks of love as a treasure hidden in a field. The task is for you each to decide what the story means for your lives. Take the last ten minutes of your time and open up a dialogue with one another. Center your dialogue on the four essential reflections of every *Lectio Divina* explained below. Use the guidelines we have included under each reflection.

Reflection 1
What Is the Text Saying in Itself?

Matthew presents Jesus as privy to the mind of God, and by speaking in parables, Jesus engages us at an imaginative level.

Parables do not offer precise formulations of concepts nor do they develop a logical flow of ideas. A parable calls our consciousness to a specific attention through the very vagueness the parable presents. It invites our minds to fill in what is missing.

Even though it leaves specific questions about God's relationship with us unanswered, it does allow the truth to seep slowly into our bones and become a part of us. Like all good storytellers, Jesus teases his listeners to investigate the latent content of the image of the treasure in the field.

Parables contain layers of meaning that are not apparent upon first exploration. The challenge is to pause and reflect, involving your mind, imagination and emotions as you penetrate the layers. These actions will bring you to a deeper understanding of the place of God in your lives.

Matthew chronicles a number of parables in chapter 13 of his Gospel, and these form one of the high points of his work. Attention is focused on the mysterious kingdom of heaven, even though the precise meaning of this phrase remains obscure and mysterious. The parables allow us to catch a few glimpses of the work of God, but the actual understanding of what Matthew is trying to convey must flow from a change of heart. It is the heart, not the intellect, that ultimately grasps the lesson.

Reflection 2
What Is God Saying to Us Personally?

God speaks to each of us in a personal way by calling us into dialogue about our lives, our destiny or our loyalty to marriage. In this way a parable becomes an invitation to open up a fresh look at our developing spirituality. It is a dynamic endeavor, for the scriptures ask us to become active in our own process of self-discovery.

This process is both peaceful and anxiety provoking. Like marital intimacy, it invites us to embrace the challenge of love freely, yet forces us to examine our most basic assumptions about how we live and love. The process is sometimes easy, sometimes unnerving.

Jesus speaks of a treasure discovered, then reburied in a field. What is he saying about your marriage? Is it the treasure around which you orient every one of your actions? Is he reminding you that you need to change your priorities?

Perhaps you need to open up these simple questions with your spouse. Perhaps your best course of action is to quietly bring about a change of heart concerning what is important (and not important) in your life.

If the time is right, a dialogue between yourself and your spouse is in order. Perhaps it is time to talk about what really motivates you as a couple. What creates your deepest bonding? What holds you together? Is your marriage a treasure whose contents remain essentially unexplored?

Perhaps the parable invites you to sell everything you possess in order to retain this treasure.

Reflection 3
What Do We Want to Say to God on the Basis of the Text?

Jesus did much of his teaching in parables, and the Gospels carry account after account of those who react to God's initiative through a change of heart as well as stiff opposition. Few remain neutral.

Dialogue between you and your spouse is likely to echo the responses described in the gospel stories. It is conceivable that your response could cause a strain or even a conflict.

Perhaps the reading will lead to a deeper silence. Maybe you want to share your unrest with one another. Perhaps one of you feels like praying but can't find the right words.

We find that couples often learn to pray at this time, and their prayer flows from the anxiety stimulated by their hearing of the word of God. Thus, prayer invites them to enter more openheartedly into the unexplored ground of love. Here they carry on a shared dialogue with the source of all love.

Reflection 4
What Difference Can This Text Make for How We Live Our Lives?

"Listen, anyone who has ears!" Jesus proclaims (Mt 13:9). His words are an invitation to react to the parable by living more authentically. The invitation for a change of heart will influence marital intimacy significantly.

Dialogue invites a couple to make some decisions regarding what to do about their lives. How are they to treat one another differently from here on? How is the hidden ground of love to evolve into concrete manifestations of its genuineness? Does that mean a multiplication of empty words of endearment, or does it mean a genuine change of heart?

Get practical: Decide how you are going to open up fifteen minutes of quality time with one another each day. Agree to implement your resolution faithfully.

Awakenings

The process of *Lectio Divina* is straightforward, and once a couple begins to get a feel for how simple it really is, they often begin to create a place for it in their lives. Allow us to describe one couple's experience as they renewed their marriage.

"Life began to change for me when I became economically successful," began a friend one day. "We always had a good companionship in this marriage, and we managed to talk a lot, but I got real depressed when I sold my business. I talked to Jennifer, but she never really knew how bad I felt. I didn't want to burden her. I figured she could use a break, after working so hard to raise our kids."

Tom is the product of a Catholic education through high school, then a state university. His aggressive behavior became the driving force behind the creation of a successful manufacturing company. A larger company offered to buy him out, so he accepted the offer, and at age fifty-three he declared himself ready to live a leisurely life.

This resolution turned into a mixed blessing, for his aggressive behavior refused to let go of him. It actually became more intense during the long hours of early retirement, since he could no longer channel his energy into hard business transactions. Idle time left him with an empty feeling, so he aimed his unhappiness at his family. His wife questioned such intensity in his relationship with her.

Tom grew up in an alcoholic family. Christmas memories present images of a drunken father and a crying mother, which underscored a familywide embarrassment about bringing friends home. Tom's bitterness was so deep that he refused to forgive his father before his death.

When asked about a spirituality, Tom is certain about two realities. He knows he is fortunate to be married to a loving wife. Her loyalty has never wavered in twenty-seven years, even though she struggles with impatience over Tom's aggressiveness.

Second, he carries a passion for social justice, and this forms the core of his spirituality. Passion for the needs of the marginalized has pushed him to invest in statewide programs for

61

the homeless. He was awarded the volunteer of the year pin for three years in a row.

His passion for justice actually legitimated his aggressiveness, and it was only when he learned to quiet down and find a more peaceful interior experience that his spirituality blossomed.

"Can you accept the idea of God as unconditional Love?" asks his healer during one of their conversations.

"It goes contrary to the way I was trained," Tom answers. "I have always been inclined that way, but that notion is foreign to everything I was ever taught about God."

"If you can accept God as unconditional Love, your life will change. You have the rest of your life to reflect on its reality."

Through a series of healing prayers during the course of his therapy, Tom took his first steps to enter into the quiet sanctuary of the heart, where he met the God of love. There, he allowed God to heal his wounds, realign his distortions, soothe his guilt about his relationship with his father and finally embrace God in a moving experience of total love. His tears flowed freely as he felt the burdens of life lift. A newly discovered love touched him at a depth he never before allowed.

"Today sets the new foundation for your life," his healer declares, "but share your experiences with your wife, and the same healing power will build a new foundation for your growth as a couple."

"Hey, listen," he asserts. "Listen. We have never really stopped talking. I share everything I'm learning with my wife, and we both benefit from it. We are moving into depths we've never had in our marriage."

"As God becomes the ground of your love," asserts his healer, "the deepening will continue. You will begin to experience the love of God as the center of everything. You will grow in ways that are impossible through your own strength."

"I'm not a scripture scholar," Tom says, "yet it seems as if we get a richness, an insight about sacred things when we need it. I feel like God speaks directly to us."

"Indeed, that is precisely what God does," his healer adds. "The same Spirit of God who wrote these stories opens your minds to the truth of what's contained in them...and your marriage changes a little at a time. In *Lectio Divina*, it is God's agenda not our own. God draws us into the heart of love."

Marital Spirituality
The Threefold Methodology

We direct many couples like Tom and Jennifer to open up their marriage to the living reality of God's love. We have digested our efforts into three concrete steps. In these steps, we observe the intermixing of the something old and the something new that slowly evolves into a healthier marriage. The three steps are:

Step 1: Quieting Down
(catching your breath)

Step 2: *Lectio Divina*
(infusing new energy into your marriage)

Step 3: Marital Process
(honest dialogue about all matters)

We will now explore each of these dimensions in some detail and present them as distinct yet intertwined pathways for opening up a marital spirituality.

Quieting Down

We teach couples that a regular process of quieting down (catching your breath) is essential because we live in a society that seems intensely busy and unfocused. If we are truly to hear the voice of God in our lives, we have to create the quiet space that is essential to any reflective activity, especially prayer. We teach them simple exercises in breathing and centering. We have included some of them in portions of this book.

Lectio Divina (new energy for your marriage) is the art of sacred reading. It is the action of listening to the word of God in the scriptures, then inviting the heart and the mind to take in their lessons.

Lectio Divina finds its origins centuries ago in the monastic movement. From its earliest days, the backbone of monasticism has been the word of God, focusing especially on the psalms.

Prior to the invention of printing, only a few books were available, including copies of the scriptures themselves, and these were found in the centers of learning: the monasteries. Only later on did they find their way into the libraries and universities.

Because texts were scarce, monks learned to read to one another, not as a way to transfer information, but as a way to savor the word of God. They read in a slow, deliberative, reverent mode, in what might seem like a labored cadence to our ears.

This formed the foundation for what became the practice of *Lectio Divina*. The practice is still alive and is recovering its rightful place as a method to foster spiritual growth. In an age of sound bites, cyberspace and an endless flow of information, a deliberative pace and quiet reflection can seem dramatically out of phase with the way our society lives. Yet that is its beauty, for it invites us to discover the riches of God's love in a way that can only take shape in solitude and quiet.

Our application of *Lectio Divina* to marriage is a simple effort to open up the riches of this ancient spiritual treasure and make it more accessible to couples. The method itself is easy to understand, and is generally made of five simple steps:

Listen to the Word of God

Reflection
What Is the Text Saying in Itself?

Reflection
What Is God Saying to Us Personally?

Reflection
What Do We Want to Say to God on the Basis of the Text?

Reflection
What Difference Can This Text Make for How We Live Our Lives?

Even though *Lectio Divina* finds its origin in the monastic life, with a little imagination, it can be applied to marriage. The first step is simple: Share the exercise with your spouse. In order to fully explore marital spirituality and its relationship to

Lectio Divina, however, we must relate it to how marriages evolve. In other words, it must relate to marital process.

Marital Process

Lectio Divina in marriage moves the couple text by text, interaction by interaction, and experience by experience into the deeper ground of love. This invites them to undertake a journey together that is both practical and profound.

It makes a marriage work better, yet often ends in nothing less than an experience of union with God. God becomes the center of shared love, while the spouses retain an essential respect for one another's differences. They usually reflect the ground of their love in a healthy marriage marked by the ability to balance out personal needs with a deep intimacy. The balance forms the foundation of a healthy spirituality as well. Marital process revolves around keeping the balance alive.

Judy Wallerstein and Sandra Blakeslee, in their study of "the good marriage," place great emphasis on the importance of this balancing process. They assert that every marriage calls upon the couple to adapt to changes that last for as long as their history. If the marriage is to mature, it must rebalance itself, and the rebalancing takes place in early marriage, during the child-rearing years and into old age.[21]

"We searched and searched for love," begins a graying husband one afternoon during coffee. His wife listens attentively. "We spent so many years looking in the wrong places. It yielded us some satisfaction, but we never seemed to satisfy our hunger for something more substantial."

"One day, the restlessness was especially pressing. I got upset about not getting what I really wanted out of this marriage, and that pushed us both to get outrageous with one another about who was to blame for the unhappiness."

"I was the first to take the risk to heal this rift," answers his wife. "I invited him to calm down. I was led to the passage in Matthew's Gospel where Jesus stands on the hillside and presents the terms of his kingdom. We were both in tears, exhausted from the exchange, crying about how we had no more strength left to blame one another."

"I began to read to him through my tears," she continues, "and the scriptures were like soothing balm. At last we found a little rest, even though we had heard this passage so many times before:

> "That is why I am telling you not to worry about your life and what you are to eat, nor about your body and how you are to clothe it. Surely life means more than food, and the body more than clothing!"
>
> (Mt 6:25)

"We both sat there in silence crying softly," she continues. We knew our life was about to change.

Chapter 3: Toward a More Sensitized Bonding

Live Action...Again

We stand, excited about what we say, yet feel naked and vulnerable in front of a group of fifty married couples. Our one-third rule seems to be holding up, for we can feel the tension from about a third of the group. They seem to be puzzled, upset, even agitated by some of our remarks about the dynamic of love. By late Saturday morning we have completed our explanation of the hidden ground of love, then ask if anyone has any questions.

"I have one," a thirtyish woman volunteers with an upraised arm. Her arm drops to a pointing motion, aimed directly at us.

"You two are really naive," she says in a hostile manner.

"OK, tell us more."

"Look, I have three small kids. I can't find five minutes to go to the bathroom without my kids knocking down the door to get my attention. Come on, now, get realistic. How can I carve out an hour a day to do those three steps you're talking about?"

Polite laughter heightens the tension in the room, telling us that her situation is not unusual.

"Any other comments?"

More laughter.

"Yes," answers a moderately overweight male, his round face slightly ruddy from some sort of outdoor work. "You people have years of training and we have none. You have plenty of time to explore all this good stuff and we have zip. You talk about spirituality and all that good stuff, but this is all new to most of us. Can't you guys get a little more practical about what we are supposed ta do? You're as bad as my minister."

His half-humorous castigation brings a hearty laugh from everyone in the room, finally breaking the tension and freeing us to continue our exposition.

"Of course we can get practical," Claudette answers. "There's a beauty in the fact that each of you is different: Each one of you will construct a style of spirituality that is unique. God calls us to be ourselves, to be honest in the ways that we create our lives. A genuine authenticity in loving is a sure sign of God's touching us."

"Process," P. J. continues, holding up four fingers on his upraised arm. "Think in terms of process. There are four processes that define, give form and shape to marital spirituality. We believe that within one of these four processes awaits a marital spirituality that makes sense for you. We are going to ask you to decide where you are, then where you want to go with your desires for a spirituality."

"Process number one," he says pointing his index finger back at the woman, "a more sensitized bonding."

"Two," he states with a V sign held high, "an experience of the sacred."

"Three, the search for the living God."

69

"Four, the contemplative marriage."

"Gee, we feel better already," says the man with the ruddy face.

The room erupts with laughter once again.

"Give us a break," P. J. continues. "Let us explain what we mean by these four processes and we think we can help you find the style that is right for you."

The Centrality of Marital Process

We enjoy this kind of exchange. If the couples care enough to ask some hard questions, then we know they are at least absorbing enough of what we say to be involved in a creative interaction.

Pointed questions force us to move our thoughts about love from the abstract to the concrete. We underscore the idea that every marriage is somewhere in process, beginning with the first stirrings of romance, then moving toward a mature and committed love.

The word *process* implies direction. Spouses begin somewhere and go somewhere. They learn to love more generously, appreciate their differences and integrate love into a definition of who they are as a couple. At times, their evolution is slow and even; at other times, tumultuous and unpredictable.

The twists and turns of marital development can remain mysterious even to the couples themselves, often catching them by surprise, stirring up puzzlement about how they can be so different after only a few years together. Process invites them to continue the search for a rewarding relationship, even when it becomes labored. It pushes them to examine the full implications of what love means for their lives.

Critical questions must be dealt with at any phase of their

history: Who am I as an individual person? Who are you as a separate self? Does our shared relationship offer each of us some quality that we lack in our separate selves? How do we balance out these dimensions?

Consequently, process confronts a couple with not only the hard questions about what love means, it invites them to seek a balance for the three critical dimensions of a marriage: *I, you* and *we*. The balance must be maintained not only for a healthy marriage, but for a healthy spirituality.

There is no one marital spirituality. There are distinct forms and variations, but the four processes we will describe in detail serve as essential groundwork for how marital spirituality grows, matures and deepens. Every process expresses a unique variation on the balance among *I, you* and *we*. Allow us to unfold the four processes in greater detail in the coming chapters.

Process 1
More Sensitized Bonding

The most appropriate place to open up an exploration of this first process is through a love story. This one unfolds not at the beginning of a marriage, but somewhere in the middle.

"I just don't get it," says Lance, "we have so much going for us. Why does the restlessness hang on so tightly when life seems so good for us?"

"I don't know, Lance," Karen answers with visible tenderness, "I don't understand it myself. I know you do the best you can."

Although Lance and Karen's marriage of fifteen years is strained at times, they have learned to talk. They often dialogue into the night, comfortable with their openness, even if their conversation yields occasional surprises and regular challenges.

"I can no longer do what you want me to do," Lance finally asserts. "I cannot create the perfect situation for you. If you want to find happiness, you'll have to find it yourself."

"I've never really asked you to make me happy, so lighten up, Lance. I'll struggle with that one myself. I invite you not to fix anything for me any more; just listen to my efforts."

Lance now breathes a sigh of relief. It is clear that their *process* is changing. He is still invited to be supportive and loving, but the burden of responsibility for Karen's happiness is placed precisely where it belongs: on her shoulders.

Although this mini love story is hardly the stuff of great novels or riveting movies, it is expressive of a maturing process within marriage. It also opens up a discernible dimension of the hidden ground of love, since any significant change in a couple's interaction opens up new challenges for love. It consequently bonds them together in an entirely new mode.

Like all couples, Lance and Karen work out their new agenda within a core of interaction that forms the central truth of who they are.

Judy Wallerstein and Sandra Blakeslee rightly assert that this central truth of who a couple is forms the inner core of family life. The core is a complex one constructed of the expectations of what spouses want from one another. These expectations carry with them the conscious or unconscious dreams of childhood and adolescence. The core also forms around a vision for the marriage: the *I,* the *you,* and the *we* of our lives: What brought us together and where are we going in the future.[22]

In order to understand each of the four processes of marital spirituality better, allow us to speak at some length about the place of the three distinct selves and how they form the foundation for our views of marriage:

I = My Distinct Self   **You = Your Distinct Self**

We = Our Shared Self

Defining My Distinct Self

In our work with marriages, we consistently bring couples back to the critical necessity of a personal grounding. "If you are not happy with yourself," we often say, "you are unlikely to be happy with each other."

This simple statement points toward one of the most fundamental realities of married life: The center of a healthy marriage is a healthy self.

As Lance and Karen discovered in early marriage, their efforts to make one another happy yielded very little. Rather than creating the happiness they both dreamed about, their efforts yielded only tension and misunderstanding.

The shift in their orientation also brought with it a redefinition of their separate selves. Karen declared that the achievement of happiness is her personal chore. Lance was relieved of the burden of unrealistic responsibility and could now foster their intimacy in a healthier way: by listening. This became his expression of a redefined self.

The solid ground of a healthy marriage is built upon the bedrock of two individuals who have come to terms with their personhood. In brief, they enjoy a level of integration of their emotional, psychological and spiritual needs, and this opens the door to the reconstruction of personal satisfaction.

They have looked inward and have dealt honestly with their attitudes about love. They have achieved a level of personal competence that affirms for them that life is a viable proposition.

Consequently, freedom governs the ways that they deal with each other. Their relationship grows because it provides sufficient space for each of them to develop their unique potentiality. Intimacy takes root in the fertile soil of self-respect, while it invites respect of spouses for one another. Consequently, their bonding is distinctly different from the kind found in early romance.

Affirming Your Distinct Self

Marriages turn as much on mutual respect as on the quest for intimacy. Affirmation of my own value must be balanced out with an affirmation of the distinct value of my spouse. One of the sobering lessons of early marriage is that not every day is a day of intimacy, nor is every exchange in marriage joyful and pleasant.

At times, the most appropriate response is simply to be respectful of the unique qualities of a spouse, then give them the space they request and be at peace with their efforts. The creation of space in a marriage is the prelude to new growth.

Lance's respect of Karen's new efforts to work for her happiness becomes an affirmation of her person. There is no greater sign of respect for a partner's integrity than to listen to them. This pure form of presence clears the way for love to mature.

Embracing Our Shared Self

The blending of my distinct self (I) and your distinct self (you) into our shared self (we) forms the essential dynamic of relating. The interplay of the three selves gives intimacy its captivating flavor and texture.

Whether the sharing is an activity, a quiet conversation, a rich experience of spirituality or an honest exchange of feelings, an embrace of the shared self bonds a couple together at the soul level. It opens up a vision of marriage for them. They now possess a more solid foundation for a spirituality. For many, this is their spirituality.

"For the first time since we have been married," Karen says, "Lance hears me. He listens to me. That helps me find my way to my own happiness."

We encourage couples to keep their minds open and their hearts undivided as they struggle to define the specifics of their interaction. In the final analysis, they gain access to the more challenging dimensions of love by achieving a balance among the three selves.

Keep in mind that developmental processes in marital spirituality take shape in a variety of ways. At one time, couples place an undiluted priority on a rich and consistent intimacy. The shared self becomes the focus and foundation of their efforts to love. The hidden ground of love becomes more visible as they become more sensitized to one another. It can seem as if growth in this kind of spirituality is effortless

Processes can shift quickly and without warning, however, and a strong emphasis on the development of the individual self becomes a consuming passion. This shift can even take place with both partners at the same time.

During this time, sharing minimizes and independence maximizes. With this change of focus, couples learn to grow by talking honestly and openly about their respective positions. Marriage during these times can bring few rewards, especially if a couple is immersed in a long bout with doubt and uncertainty about what they want from one another.

Even here, however, the emergence of the hidden ground of love is real, for spouses are learning to respect and value one another. For every couple the process of balancing, unbalancing and rebalancing the three selves continues until their history is finished.

You are also somewhere in process in your marriage. We invite you to examine the interplay of the three selves within your relationship in order to become more conscious of your unique process of spirituality.

Allow us to return to the three steps in spiritual development we discussed earlier:

Quieting Down
Lectio Divina
Marital Process

We will highlight each of these three steps and ask you to reflect on your developing spirituality. Hopefully, our efforts will move you toward a more sensitized bonding.

Quieting Down

Take some personal time and be alone. We mean really alone, all by yourself, without the usual distractions of a busy family life. On an afternoon when your family is gone, open up an hour just to be alone and begin to cultivate the fertile ground of your own soul. Breath easily as you prepare the fertile ground of your soul for the reception of God's word. In this *Lectio Divina,* we return to St. Matthew's Gospel and his account of Jesus teaching in parables.

Lectio Divina:
The Three Selves in Your Marriage

That same day, Jesus left the house and sat by the lakeside, but such crowds gathered round him that he got into a boat and sat there. The people all stood on the beach, and he told them many things in parables. He said, "Imagine a sower going out to sow. As he sowed, some seeds fell on the edge of the path, and the birds came and ate them up. Others fell on patches of rock where they found little soil and sprang up straight away, because there was no depth of earth; but as soon as the sun came up they were scorched and, not having any roots, they withered away. Others fell among thorns, and the thorns grew up and choked them. Others fell on rich soil and produced their crop, some a hundredfold, some sixty, some thirty. Listen, anyone who has ears!"

(Mt 13:1–9)

What Is the Text Saying in Itself?

Matthew places a special importance on the message of Jesus by portraying him as a master teacher. He is surrounded by such a large crowd that he must search for a conspicuous place from which to deliver his message. Thus, Matthew places him in a boat, with the crowd lining the beach, eager to hear from him.

Even though the images of seeds, rocky ground and fertile soil are familiar to an agrarian audience, the images are universal enough in their appeal that the point is easily taken. Several verses later, Matthew tells us that the seed is literally the word of God, and the seed lives or dies according to the ground that receives it.

> "The one who received it on patches of rock is the man who hears the word and welcomes it at once with joy. But he has no root in him, he does not last; let some trial come, or some persecution on account of the word, and he falls away at once."
>
> (Mt 13:20)

In brief, the parable speaks to Jesus' listeners about the ways that the word of God is heard, absorbed and made a part of life. The word dies or flourishes according to the heart of the listener.

What Is God Saying to Us Personally?

Let your imagination carry you into a relationship with the God who gives life as you place yourself on the shore of the lake as a member of the large crowd of listeners.

Is your heart open to receiving the word of God? Are you there alone, or are you with your spouse? Does your presence or notable absence to one another mean that your expectations about marriage are changing?

Do you look at marriage as a gift from God—an expression of God's word? Does God's word fall on the rocky ground of your heart, or does it find a home in the fertile soil of a growing compassion?

Does the interpersonal atmosphere of your marriage

resemble the ground covered with thorns? Is your intention to remain closed to a deeper self-disclosure and thereby choke off the possibilities for growth in new love? Does the intensity you carry to preserve your individual self under all circumstances place you in a closed position? Have you actually deadened your own life by becoming inflexible?

What Do We Want to Say to God on the Basis of the Text?

Perhaps this is the time for prayer. Perhaps it is a time to remain silent and simply be grateful for the abundance of gifts that God offers to you and to your beloved.

Maybe it is a time to rejoice in the ways that the seed of love has grown in your marriage, from its uncertain beginnings to a mature respect for your spouse. Perhaps it is a time to praise God for the times when the rocky ground of self-doubt, angry feelings and burning resentments gave way to a greening of forgiveness.

Perhaps it is time to ask God to give you the help you need to open up your life together in fresh ways: develop a new vitality, remind one another of your dreams, express your deepest longing for tenderness.

Maybe it is time to simply share a feeling of gratitude for the unbreakable bond of love that sustains you during times of doubt, uncertainty, even conflict.

What Difference Can This Text Make for How We Live Our Lives?

The last part of the parable reminds us that God deals in abundance, for the remarkable part of the narrative is that in every respect growth takes place, if even for a short period of time. When the heart is open to hear the word of God, growth is measured in superabundance.

Jesus explains the explosion of growth that takes place in the last lines of the parable:

> "And the one who received the seed in rich soil is the man who hears the word and understands it; he is the one who yields a harvest and produces a hundredfold, now sixty, now thirty."
>
> (Mt 13:23)

The great promise of the parable is that of an ever growing abundance of life, and abundance flows from an open heart. In marriage, an effort to develop a more sensitized bonding gives form and character to a spirituality grounded in a soil of openness, generosity and respect.

This example of new abundance in love comes from a couple who welcomed the blossoming of new respect for one another. It developed after a long and painful effort to assert their individual selves. They finally achieved a balance among their three selves, and their relationship matured significantly:

"Sometimes, I sit in silence and admire her beauty," he says. "I'm really awed by the fact that she loves me. I feel this respect and gratitude within me, but I can't always express it."

"We've both learned to respect each other's differences," he continues. "She confronts me about my passivity, and I jostle her about not overreacting. Our differences balance themselves out."

"Most of the time, we respect each other," she says. "We will never be the same. We have learned to be more quiet and respectful instead of forcing change. We live in the realization that God loves us both, even though that means a different experience for each of us."

Fullness in a marriage evolves slowly, experience by experience, as a couple tills the ground of their relationship, searching for and savoring the abundance that God offers them. The balancing out of *I, you* and *we* take continued effort and great sensitivity.

Into the Hidden Ground of Love

The journey into the hidden ground of love is a journey of the individual self as much as it is a journey toward intimacy. Entering freely as a couple into the mystery of love offers a dimension to a marriage that no other form of growth touches. Marriage encompasses the struggle to live with pettiness or to deal with the hard questions of belonging and separateness. The struggle brings out the best or the worst in us.

Although they speak of the journey of marriage in primarily psychological terms, Judy Wallerstein and Sandra Blakeslee underscore the fact that the qualities of love and empathy are what build the foundation for a good marriage.[23]

The more a couple lives a life of deep empathy and selfless love, the more they enter into the life of God. God is love, and the uniqueness of God's love is expressed in the amazingly different stories of the journey.

Some couples chart their course early in their history, then continue it in a confident fashion. They arrive at precisely that ground of love where they are comfortable in staking out their claim, then remain solidly ensconced in a home they both love.

Others enter the ground in spite of themselves, sometimes searching for years to find a meaning to the twists and turns that life takes for them. After much travail and doubt, they find a rich existence in a place they never believed they would inhabit.

Love inevitably brings its reward and makes its demands. The couple discovers quickly that if they desire depth, they can turn toward the depths of love itself. They hunger for union with God, and God embraces them in return.

More Live Action

P. J. stands in front of the same group of couples, continuing his efforts to turn over the hidden ground of love for them.

"Let's all open our eyes, today," he says. "What we see so often among married couples is a gold mine of wisdom they are usually reluctant to talk about. So many feel like second-class citizens because they cannot articulate their experiences like a trained religious."

A few heads nod in agreement. The discussion has now come full circle, back to the couples themselves, as we ask them to sharpen and integrate the spirituality that many of them already live. It is another affirmation, as depicted in the parables, that God deals in abundance. The abundance becomes apparent as we ask these couples to share what is already alive within their relationships.

"Just for fun," P. J. continues, "let your thoughts run free. Let's tap the reservoir of wisdom right now; tell me, what are the lasting qualities of love that somehow open up the hidden ground of love for you?"

Silence, then an unknown face takes the first risk.

"Sensitivity to the bond we possess," she says.

"Caring, sharing, tenderness," another voice adds.

"Listening, always listening."

"Paying attention to one another."

"Taking each other seriously."

"Respect and friendship."

The ideas flow freely: empathy, care, honesty, affirmation, compassion.

P. J. holds his arm up for the avalanche to stop.

"Now," he asks, "what do these qualities all have in common?"

"They are all different ways of saying the word love," someone remarks.

"Right," he answers, "and each one of these qualities marks a specific geography of the hidden ground that will open to you as you become more sensitive to one another. Sensitivity marks the domain of God, and for all of us now in this complicated and overly busy life, this is the closest we will ever get to knowing what God is like. Married love is God's clear presence to us."

Toward a Sensitized Bonding

Allow us to return briefly to the mini love story of Lance and Karen. Their reprioritizing will bring them to a fullness in love they could never have discovered while they were busy being overly responsible for one another's growth.

"I found out what it means to hear someone," Lance says. "Once I decided I was out of the business of trying to make Karen happy, it seemed to make life a lot easier. I am free to hear what she is really feeling, and I am more composed when she struggles to find her place in life, her happiness.

"Forgiveness," Karen answers, "used to come with such difficulty; now it seems so much easier. I'm no longer upset with him for trying to control me. I can forgive so much more easily now that I have some space."

Forgiveness keeps their vision alive. They carry a renewed sense of trust for one another. It allows them to leave behind their fears, denials, reservations, unclarity, alienation and move ever more securely toward a grounding in love that is open-ended.

Marriage invites them to transcend the hardness of life and live free of the pain of alienation. It also invites them to share their love through ever expanding circles of life-giving activity. It opens out into a romance with the universe. It speaks to them of a destiny in the stars. It is as if the bond between them expands their awareness into cosmic dimensions.

John Welwood, a current spokesperson for this romantic view of love, suggests that a growing love must have a focus outside the couple if they are to survive. He insists that the larger arc of a couple's love must establish a feeling of kinship with all of life. His vision of love becomes cosmic when he declares that only a love of the universe can insure that a couple's love will "develop in boundless light and power."[24]

Because the quality of interaction is the central focus of their lives, a couple living out the process of a more sensitized bonding may or may not find room for a personal God. For many, it makes no difference. The growth of their love is the primary measure of a rich union, and this moves them toward the love that they actively seek to bring to fulfillment.

Although this process is the most concrete of the spiritualities for couples, it can be problematic. Its more popular forms are aimed solely at feeling good. The vision of marriage can be narrow. Books that promise "ten easy steps to a fulfilling relationship" are misleading. They are too focused on problem solving. They foster the impression that if a couple simply incorporates a series of problem solving techniques, they will arrive at a fulfilling relationship. Many couples discover that even though the problem solving can be helpful, it does not lead them to a soul connection.

We often find couples, for example, who are highly skilled in their use of technique, but they lack the "feel" for deep relating. They are observably lacking in compassion. Although they are technically precise, their marriages tend to be stiff, suspicious and closed to the larger questions of love. In brief, they are looking for life in the wrong place.

We also know couples who desire a connection with the hidden ground of love but are so fearful of an honest exploration of these matters that they only dabble in deeper truths. They mouth the language of love but never really become vulnerable and open with one another.

Spirituality for them is confused with an effort to "feel good." They refuse to explore the deeper questions of love: What does their relationship have to do with the quest for God? What meaning does spirituality give to the inevitable periods of darkness, dryness or conflict that are part of any marriage? Does their love have anything to do with the presence of God as unseen partner? Are they called to worship jointly as well as feel good?

Lectio Divina:
Opening to New Sensitivity

"The kingdom of heaven is like the yeast a woman took and mixed in with three measures of flour till it was leavened all through."

(Mt 13:33)

What Is the Text Saying in Itself?

Leaven in Jewish society was interpreted as the symbol of evil. Here, Jesus takes this symbol and reframes it as a symbol of good. For our purposes, this parable offers another deep insight into the hidden ground of love and how this reality can subtly transform life. Like yeast, love can seem small and powerless at times, yet it surely and quietly transforms, elevates and heals in such a way that its presence is unmistakable.

God's living presence, like the leaven Jesus describes, works quietly beneath the surface of day-to-day interaction, raising it to fullness. Its manifestation can lift our spirits and deepen our intimacy in surprising ways.

What Is God Saying to Us Personally?

Take risks? Develop a broader view? Learn that the source of a genuine sensitivity to one another comes from an awareness of God's love for us? Trust what love promises? Learn to see God in all our exchanges? All genuine sensitivity flows from respect—a balance of I, you and we? Our efforts to love are not done in isolation? God is there in the deepest center of our being, working in conjunction with our good will to bring our marriage to life?

What Do We Want to Say to God on the Basis of the Text?

Get practical. Write out a plan of action that incorporates two concrete resolutions about the ways you will trust one another. Make sure you incorporate a regular dialogue about your vision of marriage into this plan of action.

Include specific efforts to share your gratitude for the gifts of your marriage. Be specific about the ways you see God bearing fruit for your life. Set aside time each day to read the scriptures, and begin the practice of prayer together. That will open up an awareness of the ways that God works with compassionate subtlety in the deep interior of your marriage.

What Differences Can This Text Make for How We Live Our Lives?

Cultivating an ever deepening realization that God works in the interior of their marriage invites a couple to see each other differently. They cannot help but respect the individual self of the spouse. They cannot help but be more sensitive to one another, and this deep sensitivity opens them to the riches of a lived spirituality.

Decide, through brief dialogue about your future, one new way that you can open up a more sensitized bond. Make it so specific that you are willing to dedicate fifteen minutes per day to its implementation.

In Summary...

For all its shortcomings, even its shortsightedness, the process of sensitized bonding can be rich and rewarding. If a couple learns, especially, to break out of an exaggerated slavery to technical precision in communicating and not be overly concerned with stiff allegiance to style, this process can be expansive.

It engenders great romantic imaginings and powerful swells of emotion as a couple expands their love toward the universe. It seems to sweep them up into a mystery greater than themselves.

Chapter 4: An Experience of the Sacred

If spouses sustain their vision of what marriage can be, do their best to deal with life in a creative fashion and stay loyal to one another through times of challenge and change, they find an inevitable deepening of their relationship. This maturing brings them into the heart of the second major process in marriage: *an experience of the sacred*.

Once the quest gets underway, the sacred yields its gifts in surprising ways. A sense of awe awaits a couple as previously disjointed elements of their interaction coalesce into a wholeness. The feeling of awe confirms that marriage is right for them. They believe in themselves and thereby trust their capacity to make marriage good and fruitful.

They swell with pride, knowing that they have lived a large segment of life together and are making marriage work. Their hearts beat with a realization that love transcends their once labored efforts to keep their relationship alive.

The hidden ground of love manifests itself not so much as the product of hard work, but as powerful moments of realization that marriage is a much bigger reality than is constructed solely through human efforts.

Growth in marriage becomes a distinctly different endeavor than that prompted by mere technique, efforts to become more sensitized to one another, or attempts to heal serious division. Too often, these efforts are external to the real heart of a marriage. The emergence of the sacred signals a true inward journey, and the soul of a marriage manifests it.

The couple stops searching for magic answers from outside themselves and invites quiet time in order to be present to one another. They listen to and learn more about each other's desires for wholeness and closeness. Love seems to emerge spontaneously, sometimes with pleasant surprise, from a foundation that reaches into the core of the couple. The sacred becomes as familiar as their own breathing.

Quieting Down: Breathing in the Sacred

We invite you to be together for a time in a quiet space: a secluded corner of your home, an open space on one of your walks, or a favorite location in your travels. Allow that familiar space to invite the sacred to come alive within you.

Breathe in once again, slowly and deliberately, realizing that the word *spirituality* finds its roots in the Latin word, *spiritus* (spirit or breath). It reflects the same notion as two words we have already explored at some length: *Ruah* (Hebrew for breath) and *Pneuma* (Greek for breath). All the great religious traditions pay homage to the significance of deep breathing, for they affirm that the breath is our connection with the sacred. We breathe it in; it becomes part of us. We become filled with spirit.

With this in mind, recall one significant time in your lives when the experience of love delivered you into the realm of the sacred. There is no mistaking its action. We breathe deeply as the sacred lifts us out of the narrow confines of life, expands our minds and fills our hearts. Sometimes an encounter with the sacred is so powerful it takes our breath away, or our chests swell with awe and respect.

Perhaps you recall a time of honest sharing in your marriage, when the barriers fell away and you really heard one another for the first time. Perhaps you remember an anniversary, when you felt especially close and loving, knowing that the hard work of marriage carried you to a sacred place you had never explored before.

Maybe it was a time when you were reeling from the reality of a loss in the family and you discovered a surprising reservoir of compassion for one another.

It can come during a simple shared experience: watching the sunrise, walking along the surf, listening to the dreams that give hope to your life.

Simply breathe slowly and give your mind the space it needs to get in touch with the sacred—the *now* of life. Allow it to slow you down, awaken you to what is real, then move you to the deeper regions of the self. Rest for a time in the goodness of life. If you are moved to do so, share your experience with your spouse.

Encounters with the Sacred

John Welwood opens up similar notions of the sacred as he reflects on the meaning of love. He describes love as an awakening that breaks us out of the sleep induced by old unconscious patterns. We awaken through love to the now of our existence. The awakening invites us into a more authentic experience of who we really are, and this becomes the basis of a healthy and satisfying relationship.[25]

If you find your awareness opening up to broad and expansive vistas, embrace it and share the experience with your spouse. Love invites you to travel to the center of this mystery. The God of love awaits your arrival. Let the simple, uncluttered reality of your love for one another become the gateway to real joy.

Encounters with the sacred are open to every couple, and the encounters become more real as a couple takes the time to slow down, move inward and learn to be sensitive to what is already unfolding in their inner selves. We are surrounded by, saturated with, enfolded in the sacred, yet seldom take the time to allow it to touch us. It invites a real awakening.

Can we understand, for example, the true nature of a rose or describe a tear or understand how human vision works? Can we define the difference between light and dark or know how an airplane flies? Can we understand what love is? Do we really know how relationships work? Can we adequately describe what happens when we fall in love?

In every one of these experiences, touched as they are by the sacred, we labor to find a description that satisfies our need to know. Instead, we stand in awe before the inexpressible.

Growth in the ways of love, then, is really an invitation to come home to an awakening to the sacred. We become aware of the powerful dynamic of love that is already working within us. Awareness of the sacredness of love invites, in turn, a radical rethinking of our very selves.

Thomas Merton, near the end of his life, sums up the place

of love in his life story, and he speaks clearly of its sacred nature. It opens out into a life of freedom and spontaneity:

> One thing has suddenly hit me—that nothing counts except love and that solitude that is not simply the wide-openness of love and freedom is nothing. Love and solitude are the one ground of true maturity and freedom...true solitude embraces everything, for it is the fullness of love that rejects nothing and no one, is open to all in all.[26]

A Deeper Marital Journey

A shift in attitudes takes place as couples begin to reinterpret marriage as a doorway into sacred ground. Few couples welcome the invitation, because it is difficult to say yes to mystery and let go of what they know as the predictability of their lives. Yet, if they desire to savor the sacred within their experiences, they must be willing to let go of their fixed and superficial views of the nature of love. The following example shows how some couples can crash hard as they make the discovery.

"By the fifteenth year of our marriage," he says, "we were solidly locked into the world of the classic yuppie couple—big house, two Mercedes in the garage, plenty of optimism about a smooth and uncluttered future."

"Correct," she says, "all our values clustered around upward mobility. Our children were precocious—the right schools and all that. We decided the timing was right to produce our third and last child, and when she was born with Down's syndrome, our world collapsed around us."

"**We were** crushed," he continues. "We didn't know which way to turn. We had such a hard time facing our friends, since they kidded us continually about another Ph.D. in the family.

The kidding was replaced by a strained silence. None of them knew what to say."

"We dropped into a terrible time of confusion and honest reevaluation, including an exploration of a spirituality that might help us find some meaning in this," she says.

"One counselor finally broke the ice by inviting us to pray with her. She directly asked God to give us the capacity to see the gift of this child. At the time, it was difficult to see this event as a gift, but now I realize that the prayer opened up something inside of us that had been dead."

"Our lovely Down's syndrome daughter is now nine years old, and such a bundle of love. Her brothers love her and take good care of her. I'm not too sure who is teaching whom. We started out to train her, and she ends up teaching us about the joy of being alive. I sometimes watch her and just cry because this child is so beautiful. She teaches us what's important in life."

Sam Keen hints at the magnitude of events of this sort by suggesting that love is so powerful that the spirit takes a giant leap forward in a realization that it is "love that moves the cosmos."[27]

Like the quickening of our breath, the sacred becomes dramatically present through a number of *signs*. Allow us to describe a few of them.

An Experience of Awe

"There is a catwalk around the edge of my observatory," a stargazer-acquaintance began, "and the first thing people on tour ask is 'why the catwalk?'"

"Before I go to work on a night's scientific project," he continues, "I walk the entire circumference of the observatory building; the catwalk runs all the way around it. I take a cloud reading and look for the best place to get an observation. The universe is so vast and spectacular. It invites powerful feelings about its grandeur and reminds me of my smallness. I feel myself standing there in awe and feel almost forcibly pulled into the spectacular mystery above me and all around me. I am drawn out of myself and into the majesty. That sense of awe is what keeps me doing astronomy."

Although marriage hardly measures up to the magnitude of this astronomer's experience, nevertheless it creates its own magic at times. Feelings of reverence, respect, admiration, trembling and fear are unmistakable signs of the sacred. They are often the feelings couples use to describe a profound sexual encounter. They also describe an unexpected clarity about love.

"I awakened one night," reports a husband, "as I can do when I'm restless, and became very conscious of my wife's slow, rhythmic breathing. I felt lots of anxiety on this coldest night of the winter. I listened to her breathing for a time, while I thought about the tenuous connection we both claim with life."

"First I got frightened," he continues, "then I began to think, 'what if she stops breathing? What if this is our last hour together? What would I say to her? What should I ask in forgiveness? If she stops breathing, is this the end of our relationship, or do we still exist in a timeless dimension?'"

"My thoughts began to run away with me and I moved toward panic, then I calmed a bit, reached over and placed my hand in hers."

"She stirred slightly," he continues. "The rhythm of her breathing changed, then she responded back by squeezing my hand. I prayed silently for her, asking God to protect her and to give us many more days together. I was visited by a powerful experience of reassurance, as if God was telling me to be at peace. I was caught up in a feeling of deep wonder that this was not an accidental moment, but that God really cares about us. Peacefulness then came quickly; it completely replaced my anxiety, and I slept soundly the rest of the night."

The Surrender of Invincibility

"Vulnerable," he says, "I never felt such vulnerability in my life. I never had a sick day in sixty-eight years, and I half-believed I would stay that healthy forever...until that first heart attack."

"I was really scared," affirms his wife. "Forty-one years of marriage and I never saw him weak or fragile. It caught me completely off guard. I never felt so vulnerable myself."

"We have been through this sort of thing with others, but never were we asked to trust God at this level. I was near death several times, but I miraculously pulled through."

"It was a time of real change. We learned to cry together, pray together, appreciate one another as gifts from God and enjoy one another's company once again. His recovery opened up a whole new view of life for us, and we have been reconfirmed in the sacredness of our love."

Love often calls upon a couple to explore the connection between life and death, the sacred and the profane, time and eternity. When the sacred opens up into an encounter with a personal God, every effort to love can bring a deeper consciousness of God's unswerving loyalty.

Honesty with One Another

Transparent honesty moves a couple into the free and spontaneous domain of relating. Their honesty expresses not just an exercise in precise language or a jolting encounter with raw unfiltered truths. It reflects two lives touched by the sacred. Once touched, they respect each other so much they cannot relate in any other way except honestly.

They show many of the same efforts at honesty we discover in the couples who develop a more sensitized bond, yet the groundwork of honesty is distinctly different. Honest exchanges flow from a genuine inner confidence in themselves, their destiny and a connection with God. This awareness frees them up to be open with one another without undue worry about a partner's reactivity.

They do not hesitate to say what needs to be said. They are open about their feelings. They temper their honesty with compassion.

The sacred ground of love gives them an anchor, a refuge, a harbor that allows them to be caring and open, yet candid and forthright. They speak from a grounding in the sacred that sustains them, knowing that their candidness is an expression of a belief that they must be honest in order for love to flourish.

Peacefulness

They each enjoy a peacefulness, because they have progressed into the deeper ground of love and have found a home there. They are open about how good their marriage is and are uncompromisingly optimistic about their future. Their interaction is reflective of the inner harmony they both enjoy. Their peacefulness is contagious, even with one another.

It matures through an awareness that every exchange of love further deepens their relationship with the sacred. All exchanges become a sign that they are journeying into the unexplored terrain of love, and this is exactly where they belong.

The cumulative effect is a simple one: they share from a

centered self and consequently enjoy a grounding in their own truth. If a reevaluation of their relationship is called for, they do it willingly.

Freedom

Freedom is not so much the liberty to enjoy an unencumbered life or to be entertained through unrestricted meanderings to exotic places as much as it is the freedom to be.

In a marriage in which a couple shares real freedom, they derive great pleasure in living a simple life together. Their communication process reflects an inner landscape that confirms both of them in their self-worth. All interaction reflects their interior sacred space because they respect and affirm one another.

Love is sacred because it removes doubts about their value as persons. The marriage begins to reflect the qualities of unconditional love that manifest the connection with the sacred. As they pursue the deeper call to love, they begin to reflect the quality of selfless love that flows only from a relationship with the God who is unconditional love.

Lectio Divina: The Ideal and the Real of Love

It seems that at almost every wedding we hear the great hymn of praise to love from St. Paul's First Letter to the

Corinthians (13:1th ff.). It presents such a lofty ideal, it seems better suited for weddings than for tenth anniversary celebrations. It also offers suitable material for *Lectio Divina*.

Find the time to be together and quiet down. Place yourself in the presence of the sacred by recalling to one another the deep spirit of love you brought to your wedding day.

Make a decision about who is to read, then one of you read the following text to the other slowly and deliberately, while you both listen once again to the vision of love that seemed close to you at one time.

Listen to the Word of God

If I have all the eloquence of men or of angels, but speak without love, I am simply a gong booming or a cymbal clashing. If I have the gift of prophecy, understanding all the mysteries there are, and knowing everything, and if I have faith in all its fullness, to move mountains, but without love, then I am nothing at all. If I give away all that I possess, piece by piece, and if I even let them take my body to burn it, but am without love, it will do me no good whatever. Love is always patient and kind; it is never jealous; love is never boastful or conceited; it is never rude or selfish; it does not take offense, and is not resentful. Love takes no pleasure in other people's sins but delights in the truth; it is always ready to excuse, to trust, to hope, and to endure whatever comes. Love does not come to an end. But if there are gifts of prophecy, the time will come when they must fail; or the gift of languages, it will not continue forever; and knowledge—for this, too, the time will come when it must fail. For our knowledge is imperfect and our prophesying is imperfect; but once perfection comes, all imperfect things will disappear. When I was a child, I used to talk like a child, and think like a child, and argue like a child, but now I am a man, all childish ways are put behind me. Now we are seeing a dim reflection in a mirror; but then we shall be seeing face to face. The knowledge that I have now is imperfect; but then I shall be known as fully as I am known.

In short, there are three things that last: faith, hope and love; and the greatest of these is love.

(1 Cor 13:1–13)

What Is the Text Saying in Itself?

The text itself clearly expresses the ideal of love by unhesitatingly elevating it to the summit of the Christian life. It is a clear statement that if the believer practices heroic virtue, yet lacks love, he or she remains an empty shell.

It also holds up an elevated prototype of how love is to be expressed (always patient and kind, never boastful, not resentful). This idealistic blueprint challenges the reader to stretch and reach to make this summit of virtue a way of life.

The text also tells us that love brings with it far deeper dimensions than simple, hard work engenders, for love forms the bridge between time and eternity. The practice of love brings us into the presence of the sacred like no other action. For now, we are asked to live with a dim vision of what life holds and love promises, but a transformation awaits those who love faithfully. The transformation will present to us a total connection with the God who is Love.

There is no question that the text puts love into a grand

perspective. Only three things last in this, our earthbound existence: faith, hope and love. Love is affirmed as the greatest of the lasting realities.

What Is God Saying to Us Personally?

The text holds up such a lofty ideal of love that some claim it is impossible to attain. Perhaps that is why it has become a favorite reading on the day of marriage: a day filled with hymns to love and testimonies to lofty ideals.

Many commentaries on the day of marriage present the text with a moral slant, by pointing toward the summit of committed lifelong love, then recount the ways spouses fail to measure up. So many reflections on the lofty ideal of love bring discouragement rather than hope.

We prefer to read it as an expression of the sacred: a statement that God's love underscores every effort we make to love our spouses. God's faithfulness allows us to move steadily toward that ideal of love, even when we don't do a very good job of loving selflessly.

It is the statement par excellence that learning to love is an immersion in the sacred. It is a promise that God will remain loyal to those who make an effort to love more honestly. They will never be without God's love. No effort to love a spouse, no matter how difficult, will go unnoticed by God.

What Do We Want to Say to God on the Basis of the Text?

That I need help in moving toward this ideal of love? That I want to enter ever more deeply into the sacred by understanding the full implications of what love means? That I need to relax a little and gain more confidence from knowing that God is with me in my efforts?

I am not alone. We are not alone. We can trust the promises that God offers, that God is with us. Perhaps it is time to pray in gratitude for the great gift of love in our lives. Even though we have not done as well as we might at times, we can live with confidence that the very ground of every effort to love is God.

Perhaps it is time to learn to pray jointly in grateful appreciation that God loves us and will bring our love to fullness. All we need is to be open. Perhaps it is time to ask God to allow you to really see what love is.

What Difference Can This Text Make for How We Live Our Lives?

Love outlasts everything: my physical life, my perceptions, my desires for affirmation and understanding. It opens out into an eternal life of love, with our marriage as the catalyst and God as the ground of this life.

This text confronts us with the reality that the dialogue of love is always a matter of learning to balance out the demands of love with the hunger for eternal union. In the human condition, the tension between time and eternity, vision and reality, present and future are never completely resolved.

Like the gospel parables suggest, God deals in abundance. The seed of God's word grows into a lush greening of our feeble efforts. God is at the center of every effort we make to love.

Marriage calls us to work hard, indeed, but the discovery of the rich bounty that unconditional love yields immerses us in sacred space. For many, it opens the way to an encounter with the personal God, who is the hidden ground of love.

As a practical exercise, spend ten more minutes discussing the aspect of love that remains the most difficult for you. Perhaps you have a difficult time remaining patient under pressure. Perhaps kindness comes all too infrequently. Perhaps you have a mean streak in you that takes a special glee in knowing that your spouse has again learned the hard way (because she didn't take your advice). Perhaps forgiveness is all too infrequent.

Each of you single out one stubborn fault you desire to change in your relationship. Admit your helplessness to one another, then ask God to give you the honesty and the strength you need to make some real changes.

Ask God to give you the desire to pray for deep healing each day. Ask to see God's presence in this struggle to love more deeply, and you'll find it much easier.

Chapter 5: Embracing the Personal God

The embrace of a personal God intensifies the drama of the search for the hidden ground of love, for marital spirituality now expresses a hunger not just for the sacred as power, energy or mysterious presence, but the sacred as *person*. This fourth process of marital spirituality literally focuses on an embrace of the God of love.

The image of God pitching a tent and living among us takes on a personal meaning, for it is God who invites the couple into the hidden ground of love. Growth in a marriage, therefore, reflects a deep dialogue between one another and with God.

The many levels of this dialogue are so intertwined that a couple discovers that as they mature in love, they learn more about the God of love. As they try to make God more real for their lives, their shared quest invites them into a powerful experience of intimacy. In a dramatic multiplication of awarenesses, they begin to understand just how surely God becomes the hidden ground of love.

The Psalms as Foundation

The Old Testament psalms yield a rich harvest of images to help us open our awareness to the reality of God's initiative in loving us. They also teach us how to respond in love.

We can touch only a few of them as we continue to explore *Lectio Divina* as a method to enrich and sustain the four processes of marital spirituality. Like delicate appetizers before an elegant meal, we hope that these few psalms will open up your appetite for more. Our examples can serve as models for the use of other psalms in your growth as couples.

The psalms have served as the backbone of Christian spirituality from the very beginning of its history. Before that, they offered substance to Hebrew worship. They form a finely woven tapestry of praise, gratitude, adoration and petition to the God who invests passionately in the affairs of ordinary people.

For married couples, a special attraction of the psalms lies in their honesty of expressiveness. They cover every human emotion, from ecstatic praise for the beauty of God's creation to outspoken hatred for the enemies of God.

Certain psalms are so expressive that they carry a shock value for the reader not accustomed to this degree of candidness in prayer. Yet, we suggest, this absoluteness of conviction is an essential part of their beauty. They invite a couple to discover the energy, the courage, the vocabulary, to express the full range of sentiment to a God who always listens, then consistently responds back.

They give couples permission to be candid in their dealings with God and one another. They invite us to enter into life as we live it, then express both its joy and suffering without reservation.

Throughout the psalms, God is presented as a God who

loves us passionately. We are invited to respond back to God with equal passion. God is called upon as the source of all life, all love, who remains loyal to us under every ambiguity, all trials. God can be trusted to remain loyal, even when close friends betray us.

The psalms present God to us through the use of powerful images: a rock, a refuge, a fortress, a gentle wind and our familiar image of a tent.

In the course of Jewish history, the meaning of the tent image and its connotation regarding our relationship with God changed and deepened. It evolved from the simple protective skin of a night campsite to God's Temple in Jerusalem. The psalms recall the image of a tent often, but the meaning deepens with use. The Temple (God's tent) became the image of the definitive dwelling place of God among God's people:

> For you will hide me in your shelter
> in the day of trouble,
> you will conceal me under the cover of your tent
> and will set me high upon a rock....
>
> (Ps 27:5)

More than any other prayer forms we have explored, the psalms invite us to explore the invisible realm of love. We usually begin our prayer day with a recitation of several of our favorite psalms. They invite us to hear the word of God, then set our priorities for the day.

We have been praying the psalms, both individually and together, for at least twenty years, so we are familiar with the rich literature of the Bible's psalter (the book of 150 psalms).

Over time, we have awakened to what we know as the rich geography of love in our marriage. It is clearly the ground of our existence, firmed up and defined by a God who cares for us with great compassion. The psalms remind us of this each day. In them, God invites us to love one another with the same compassion and intensity as God loves us. We know this is our calling. What that calling means continues to change as our bond matures.

In other words, the psalms give form, direction, substance and motivation to us to explore the full implications of what it means to live a life of love.

They clearly served the same function in the life of Jesus, for the New Testament authors place the psalms on his lips throughout his public ministry, passion, death and resurrection. They reflect his struggle to know the full implications of love for his life. Some of his last recorded words as he died, were quotes from the psalms:

> My God, my God, why have you deserted me?
> Far from my prayer, from the words I cry?
> (Ps 22:1; Mk 15:33)

Allow us to return again to the three steps in marital growth: quieting down, *Lectio Divina* and a reflection on marital process. This time we will place an emphasis on the psalms as well as a few more sections of the Gospels, in hopes that you will awaken to the presence of God in your lives.

Psalm 139 is a song of praise for the loving God, and it offers a good place to begin a reflection on the tender love of God.

Quieting Down

Find your secluded space and spend a few moments quieting down. Invite your spouse to be present with you. A simple reflection from Psalm 46 can help you find your quiet center once again: "Pause awhile and know that I am God." (Ps 46:10 JB) Repeat it slowly as you notice your breathing slowing down.

Once you have quieted down, begin your reflection with a slow reading from Psalm 139; think about what God is saying to you. Note that we have broken up the psalm into sections and offer a slight variation on the *Lectio Divina* reflections. Feel free to be equally creative as you read other psalms.

Lectio Divina:
Listen to the Word of God

Yahweh, you search me and know me.
You know if I am standing or sitting.
You perceive my thoughts from far away.
Whether I walk or lie down, you are watching;
you are familiar with all my ways.

Before a word is even on my tongue, Yahweh,
you know it completely.
Close behind and close in front you hem me in,
shielding me with your hand.
Such knowledge is beyond my understanding,
too high beyond my reach.

Where could I go to escape your spirit?
Where could I flee from your presence?

If I climb to the heavens, you are there;
there, too, if I sink to Sheol.

If I flew to the point of sunrise—
or far across the sea—
your hand would still be guiding me,
your right hand holding me.

If I asked darkness to cover me
and light to become night around me,
that darkness would not be dark to you;
night would shine as the day

(Ps 139:1–12)

What Is the Text Saying in Itself?

The psalmist sings a song of praise, and thereby fosters an awareness of a God who is so intimate with us that God knows every thought, every feeling, each desire of our being.

God is, in fact, all-knowing. God knows our most intimate thoughts even before we complete them. God's intimacy extends to a loving protection. God shields us from harm. Thus, we are the product of God's creative love, for God breathes into us the breath of life.

The writer confesses that these thoughts are too profound for him to understand. He can only stand in awe before the sacred.

With that in mind, now read the next section of the text to one another as you listen to the description of how tenderly God creates us. Our very being is the product of an artist—God, who forms us with detailed attention to the smallest aspects of our existence.

You created my inmost being
and knit me together in my mother's womb.

For all these mysteries—
for the wonders of myself,
for the wonders of your works—
I thank you.

You know me through and through
from having watched my bones take shape
when I was being formed in secret,
woven together in the womb

(Ps 139:13–15)

What Is God Saying to Us Personally?

Share with one another how this section touches you.
Perhaps you can recall an experience in which you suddenly
became aware of the presence of God in your life, one that
changed the ways you feel about one another. Perhaps it was
an experience where God broke through your crystallized
manner of doing things and made you suddenly aware that
God governs your life in ways you had never thought about.
Perhaps you became aware of how passionately God wants to
love you and to have a relationship with you.

Share a meaningful incident of this sort with one another.
Talk about how it feels. See if you can weigh the implications
of this for how you might open up your life more fully to the
hidden ground of love.

What Do We Want to Say to God on the Basis of the Text?

This psalm immerses us in a reflection on the love of God,
who creates us with great tenderness and genuine care. It can

be easily read as an expression of the same tender love that creates us in marriage. The simple action of standing in awe before this profound truth can move a couple to prayer.

We find it almost universal that couples have a hard time finding the right words to say as they struggle to define what prayer will mean for them. They generally tell us that they are not schooled in prayer, so they look for whatever aid they can find to help them become more spontaneous.

We often turn them toward the psalms, asking them to read until they find one they like, then to put themselves in the place of the psalmist while they open up their hearts. They find that it works for them, because the psalms reflect a full range of human sentiment. They place on the lips of the reader every desire of the heart, every hunger for union with God.

Return again to Psalm 139 and read this segment to one another as a prayer. A slow, reflective, prayerful reading will move you to a spirit of gratitude and praise.

> You have seen my every action;
> all were recorded in your book—
> my days determined
> even before the first one began.
> God, your thoughts are mysterious!
> How vast is their sum.
> I could no more count them
> than I could count the sand!
> And even if I could,
> you would still be with me.
>
> (Ps 139:16–18)

Perhaps your imagination can take it from there, and under the guidance of God's Holy Spirit, you can allow your spirits to pray from a foundation that is your own. We find that an easy transition to spontaneous prayer takes place if we begin our reflections with the psalms.

What Difference Can This Text Make for How We Live Our Lives?

This same psalm captures the intensity of the author's change of heart. It might seem unusually harsh for a prayer, but we want to present the entire psalm, not sanitize it. The language says a great deal about how seriously the psalmist treats a conversion experience.

Even if it seems foreign to you, try looking at it as an expression of conviction, direction and focus. The author's world is clearly divided between those who love God and those who are God's enemies. He declares his position with those who love God, and this declaration sets him at odds with those who live with evil.

> God, if you would only destroy the wicked!
> They speak evil about you,
>   regard your thoughts as nothing.
> Yahweh, I hate those who hate you
>   and loathe those who rise against you.
> I hate them with a total hatred;
>   they are my enemies, too.
> God, search me and know my heart;
>   probe me and know my thoughts.
> Make sure I do not follow evil ways,
>   and guide me in the way of eternal life.
>   (Ps 139:19–24)

Look beyond the strong language. Ask yourselves if you might share some of this purity of direction in order to alter your life. What if your desire to love each other consumed your imagination in this way, and you focused your passion with a similar intensity?

When God becomes the ground of love in a marriage, God is more than a simple ideal or a "feel good" image. God becomes intimately involved in each exchange of love, every effort to grow, each desire to be close and tender. As we say so often to our couples, God becomes the hunger, substance, form, style and source of all love.

God becomes a faithful Presence who is with us through the greatest joys and most intense suffering life holds. Each exchange between a couple and God intensifies the hunger to know more about God. God, in turn, longs to know us more intimately.

The drive is manifested in a maturing style of marital spirituality that brings a couple to a totally involving intimacy with God and with one another. The following example from a couple's life illustrates how powerfully God works during a dark time in a marriage. Everything this couple discovers about themselves, their love and their future is echoed in almost identical words in a psalm.

"I just couldn't seem to get it together," he says. "I was done: demoralized and empty. I had just suffered a big loss— my dad's death, a month before. I didn't think I could take any more loss; then my wife announced that she wanted out of the marriage."

"I sat in intense despair on the edge of my bed and felt like praying, but just couldn't find the right words. All I could think of was that prayer of Jesus on the cross: 'My God, my God, why have you forsaken me?' I couldn't even remember where to find it, or how the rest of it goes, so I just sat there and repeated it, hitting the word *me* real hard. I started to slide the wedding ring off my finger, knowing it was all over. The ring came half off, but then a powerful intuition told me that I should leave it on because we still had enough loyalty left in us to make this marriage work."

"I slid it back on," he continues. "I knew that my dogmatic old self had to die. I had no choice. It took quite a while for me to find the courage, but my wife and I began to talk honestly for the first time in years. The marriage changed."

It took this man several months and a lot of prayers to get to the level of honest conversation that he needed to open up his marriage. The opening began with a gentle nudge from God, who invited him to not only reevaluate his style of communicating, but to accept a total healing of his attitudes.

He set himself on a course of spiritual development by actually learning to read the psalms and enjoy them. He has frequently asked his wife to open up a shared effort at prayer, but she is reluctant to be that vulnerable. Nevertheless, they continue to heal their marriage.

The story also illustrates a renewal of several qualities that are essential for a healthy marital spirituality. Allow us to name several of these qualities and suggest how they are a vital dimension in the quest for the living God. They are a concrete expression of marital process.

Marital Process:
Deepening Reflectivity

The couple enters into a *deliberately reflective mode* for a simple reason: They desire to establish a relationship with the personal God as ground of love. This shared passion invites an exploration of who God is, how this relationship can be developed, how it might mature and what may be a couple's final destiny.

"I spent the first twenty years of our marriage interested only in the externals of life," says a wife during an unguarded moment. She offers this digest of her process during a coffee break at a couples' workshop. Her spontaneity stimulates her husband's honesty.

"True enough," he says, "we were consumed with image, status, possessions, all the things that make for a very typical middle-class life."

"The only problem—it consumed us," she says. "We ended up looking very successful, but lacked substance for our marriage. It finally got to us—the emptiness. There were no great revelations that brought us to examine the importance of change—just an emptiness that never seemed to go away. Boredom with one another eventually killed our desire to go on like this. Our achievements couldn't feed our souls."

"Change? When did it come? How did it evolve? I'm not too sure. It just seemed to evolve. The hunger for something greater pushed us into the beginnings of thoughtfulness, inwardness. We began to explore some hard questions about what life really means, and this exploration brought us to a different place. We both began to meditate, talk a lot more honestly about our views and try to stay open to new ideas, new ways of enriching life."

A Love of Shared Prayer

When the hunger for God drives a couple to a personal encounter with God, a love of shared prayer awaits them. They open themselves to the riches contained in the scriptures and other source materials. Their deepening consciousness of the dynamic of God's love becomes an orienting center for their lives. Prayer nourishes them. It keeps their vision alive. Marriage almost effortlessly changes into a shared journey of the soul.

We return to the psalms each morning as we begin our day. This is a welcome exercise of *Lectio Divina* within our life context. We derive great joy, enjoy a beautiful sharing and find a clear sense of direction for our lives through this process, yet we realize that our process might not be right for every couple.

We know of couples who follow structured readings from a book of daily devotions, then share their meaning with one another. Others benefit from new literature, engaging poetry or contemporary writings about marriage. Each couple derives great richness from their efforts and often moves to a prayer life that is meaningful to them.

As good as many contemporary readings are about the joys of marriage, however, we still encourage couples to mine the riches awaiting them in the scriptures. We believe that the consistent digesting of the word of God in *Lectio Divina* opens up a couple's encounter with the living God. They begin to know a God who is central to their existence. Prayer brings with it an awareness that is more than knowledge about God; this is an encounter with Love itself.

We never fail to walk away from our daily encounters with God in *Lectio Divina* more enlightened, better focused and frankly awed by God's special concern for the smallest details of our life.

A Sense of God's Unique Love for Them

Shared prayer focuses a couple on an awareness that God is a *God for them*. Thus, their experience of God moves to a deeper level. They declare that they enjoy a destiny that is not

116

only initiated, but directed and fostered by God. God leads them into the dimensions of love for which they hunger, and this deepening love becomes the most authentic sign they know that God is directing their lives.

Like a special personal friendship that is marked with thoughtful gestures, messages of concern and small signs of tenderness, God reaches out and embraces the couple. God sends special signs of God's love, and they are unmistakable. One seasoned couple shared this information with us.

"We met when we were so very young," he says. "We actually met in grade school, but of course didn't really get serious about one another until later on."

"Not much later, since you wanted a relationship with me; I remember."

"It didn't take long, really," he continues. "We felt so good about each other. We just sort of grew up together and loved God at the same time. We couldn't separate the two. We were in the Methodist youth group together."

"Forty years later, it still is right for us," she continues. "We love one another deeply. We still pray, making God the center of our lives, but it is so much deeper. God is loyal to us in a very personal way—so loyal I can't really talk about it very good. Too many times God has joined us at that real deep level—spirit or soul or something like that."

"She's correct. It seems like if we stray from our destiny, God pulls us back. We pray the 23d Psalm each day—you know: 'The Lord is my shepherd, I lack nothing. In meadows of green grass he lets me lie. To the waters of repose he leads me; there he....'"

"Jack, I'm sure the man knows the prayer; you don't need to say the whole thing for him."

"Sorry, it means a lot. You can see we have our different views."

Couples like this are acutely sensitive to one another in all matters and unpretentious in their efforts to speak about their spirituality. They embrace one another as a reflection of God's embrace.

Always Balancing the Three Selves

Husbands and wives experience God differently, yet value these very differences as a source of enrichment. They know that God speaks a different language to each of them. This leads to an increasing respect for one another's individual processes. Hence, the distinct self of each of them matures. The *I*, the *you* and the *we* develop through the creative tension that is characteristic of a good marriage.

"I simply respect her privacy," he says. "She writes a journal each morning, then she leaves it on the desk top, and it stays there. I wouldn't dare read it because these are her private thoughts."

"I respect him the same way," she says. "He has a right to his private thoughts. If he wants to share them, I'm always willing to listen. I never intrude where I don't belong."

"Nevertheless," she continues, "we have the most beautiful sharing at times. We just seem to know when it is time to open up with one another, and God blesses our efforts."

*Deepening...*Lectio Divina

We invite you to use any of the following exercises in *Lectio Divina* to infuse new life into your marriage. Feel free to focus on the one that speaks clearly to you. Each of them is constructed to open up an awareness of the personal God as central to a deep love.

Lectio Divina:
A Song of Praise

Psalm 103 is a song of praise. Place yourselves in a quiet place and listen to it. Perhaps one of you could read it to the other, then you both can sit quietly and absorb its meaning. Listen for the ways that this song is manifested in your marriage. In order to capture its entire beauty, we will include the whole psalm.

It is important to understand that as you read the scriptures, you are being transformed into loving in the same way as God loves: selflessly and openly. We call that unconditional love.

Listen to the Word of God

Bless Yahweh, O my soul.
Bless God's holy name, all that is in me!
Bless Yahweh, O my soul,
and remember God's faithfulness:
in forgiving all your offenses,
in healing all your diseases,
in redeeming your life from destruction,
in crowning you with love and compassion,
in filling your years with good things,
in renewing your youth like an eagle's.

Yahweh does justice
and always takes the side of the oppressed.
God's ways were revealed to Moses,
and Yahweh's deeds to Israel.
Yahweh is merciful and forgiving,
slow to anger, rich in love;
Yahweh's wrath does not last forever;
it exists for a short time only.
We are never threatened, never punished
as our guilt and our sins deserve.

As the height of heaven over earth
is the greatness of Yahweh's faithful love
for those who fear God.
Yahweh takes our sins away
farther than the east is from the west.
As tenderly as parents treat their children,
so Yahweh has compassion on those who fear God.

Yahweh knows what we are made of;
Yahweh remembers that we are dust.
The human lasts no longer than grass,
lives no longer than a flower in the field.
One gust of wind, and that one is gone,
never to be seen there again.

But Yahweh's faithful love for those who fear God
lasts from all eternity and forever,
so too God's justice to their children's children,
as long as they keep the covenant
and remember to obey its precepts.

Yahweh has established a throne in the heavens
and rules over all.
Bless Yahweh, all angels,

mighty in strength to enforce God's word,
attentive to every command.
Bless Yahweh, all nations,
servants who do God's will.
Bless Yahweh, all creatures
in every part of the world.
Bless Yahweh, O my soul.

(Ps 103)

What Is the Text Saying in Itself?

Some suggest the psalmist wrote this prayer as a song of thanksgiving for recovery from a serious illness. Its themes of praise highlight God as compassionate and loving, and invite us to ground ourselves in this love. The prayer is literally filled with concrete descriptions of the myriad ways that God is loyal to those whom God loves. God's love fills us with joy, it renews our youth. It lasts for all eternity.

What Is God Saying to Us Personally?

We invite you to take this psalm and use it as a source to open up your awareness of how good God is to you in your marriage. Invite your spouse to spend twenty minutes with you while you read the psalm to one another. We have already mentioned that it appears to be a prayer offered during a time of major healing: therefore, it is a prayer of gratitude.

Slowly read the lines of the psalm to one another. Stop after each line and try to name the ways that God continues "filling your years with good things," or "forgiving all your offenses." By making an effort to name all the ways that God fills your life, you will move toward a spirit of gratitude.

121

If you cannot recall the ways that God has touched your life, pause for a while and simply be quiet, catching your breath while you breathe in the presence of God. Be at peace for a time. Sometimes, the best response to God's love is simply to wait as God touches your heart in subtle ways.

What Do We Want to Say to God on the Basis of the Text?

A respectful silence in one another's presence is a genuine form of prayer. Sometimes, the inner energy of encountering God easily moves a couple into spontaneous prayer. If that is the case, then allow your prayerfulness to break free and share it with one another.

If nothing seems to be happening, try this: take the scriptures and find your way to the Book of Psalms. It's located about the middle of the Old Testament, in the center of the wisdom literature, between the Book of Job and the Book of Proverbs.

Each of you read silently from the Book of Psalms. Let your thoughts and feelings begin to germinate as you become familiar with a specific psalm that speaks to you. Settle on one that you want to share with your partner.

Invite him/her to listen to you read. Read it aloud, then express to your partner what the prayer means to you. Allow your spouse to share in return. Stay with the sharing for as long as you desire.

What Difference Can This Text Make for How We Live Our Lives?

Make a practical resolution about spending some time each day in one another's presence. We see so many marriages wither up and die because couples really believe that they are so busy they have no quality time for one another.

Fifteen minutes well spent is a lot of time, especially if it is aimed at helping one another open up to God's love. Try reciting a portion of the psalms to one another. You might be surprised at how much a simple *Lectio Divina* can change your life. If a phrase from the psalms catches your fancy, write out the phrase and place it on your mirror. You can repeat it often during the day, and it will slowly become a part of you. You will discover times when you awaken to an awareness that God's Spirit is actually praying a phrase from the psalm while you are busy with life.

The Place of Justice

The Gospels confront us with a radically different quality of married love than is found in contemporary literature. They break us out of the narrowness of simply feeling good or obsessing over the magic of closeness. They invite a couple to open up to the world in a spirit of justice.

Married love becomes a window through which a couple views the world much more critically, for the hunger for justice is an expression of their hunger for God.

We value our friendship with one such committed couple, who live a life centered in a passion for justice. They enjoy their five children, are each busy with separate professional lives, yet foster a sincere and burning passion for social change. Their passion is fueled by the Gospels.

He is an attorney, working scrupulously to provide honest service to his clients. She works part-time in a hospice as a social worker, writes a column on spirituality for the diocesan newspaper and heads a state organization chartered for the sole purpose of eliminating the death penalty.

After twenty-one years of marriage, they are still deeply in love. Their marriage has matured into an oasis each enjoys when in need of rest. They work hard to be sensitive and loving to one another. They enjoy their process of continued growth. Their shared dialogue, firmly grounded in prayer, brings them consistently back to the central place of love.

Love gives them the security to reach out to others in the works of justice. Thus, marital process, a deepening passion for justice and a vision for their future are all intertwined. One builds upon the other.

Refocusing through the Gospels

When a couple seeks to anchor their lives in the hidden ground of love, they enter terrain already explored and marked in the life of Jesus.

Matthew's Gospel offers insight into the struggles of Jesus to live a vision of love, clearly describing his efforts in the drama of the temptations in the desert. Matthew places this event at the beginning of Jesus' ministerial life.

Jesus is portrayed as one who makes an effort to keep the great commandment alive:

> Listen, Israel: Yahweh our God is the one Yahweh. You shall love Yahweh your God with all your heart, with all your soul, with all your strength. Let these words I urge on you today be written in your heart.
>
> (Dt 6:5)

Jesus wrestles with difficult questions, each one of them inviting him to focus on the priorities in his life, his mission and his awareness of what a call from God means.

In *Lectio Divina,* the life of Jesus becomes not only a blueprint for seeking justice, but a believable example for married couples to get their priorities straight. If we are to enter into a mature union with God, we are called on to refocus our lives on what matters and to discard whatever becomes a distraction. To live in the hidden ground of love is to live with an undivided heart.

Lectio Divina:
Getting Our Priorities Straight

Sit together and quiet down once again. Come into the presence of God as you find your center. Prepare yourselves to listen to the word of God once again. St. Matthew begins to speak of the struggle of Jesus in this fashion:

> Then Jesus was led by the Spirit out into the wilderness to be tempted by the devil. He fasted for forty days and forty nights, after which he was very hungry; and the tempter came and said to him, "If you are the Son of God, tell these stones to turn into loaves." But he replied, "Scripture says: "Man does not live on bread alone but on **every w**ord that comes from the mouth of God.""
>
> (Mt 4:1–5)

What Is the Text Saying in Itself?

Matthew likens Jesus' forty days in the desert to the wandering of the chosen people described in the Old Testament Book of Exodus. Their wandering in the desert between Egypt and the Promised Land became a time of great purification. The psalms are replete with accounts of the wandering in the desert and what that meant for their national consciousness.

Since Matthew was writing primarily for a Jewish audience, he presents Jesus as the new Moses, seeking the solitude of the desert during a time of purification. Although the parallels between the lives of Jesus and Moses are striking, the struggle of Jesus is unique.

Matthew presents the forty days of Jesus in the desert as a time of great personal purification. The image of the desert becomes symbolic of his inner desolation and emptiness. We usually describe this imagery as explicating a psychological journey through the desert. Jesus seeks solitude while under the pressure of hard questions about his ministry, then emerges with a more clearly defined awareness of his own personhood.

Jesus quotes the Old Testament Book of Deuteronomy to his detractor. It invites the people of God to rely solely on God and to live in absolute trust of God's generosity. By quoting this passage, Jesus clearly rejects the temptation to live with a divided heart.

What Is God Saying to Us Personally?

The development of a good marriage is richly rewarding, but it also has the quality of the desert about it. Daily routine, uncertainty about the future, chronic misunderstandings and unexpected losses all challenge a couple to adapt to the reality of a shared life. Efforts to find a temporary fix for problems or to live a superficial life do not satisfy the deeper hungers of the heart. Jesus simply states that we do not live by bread alone, but by the word of God.

Look at your own lives and find the parallels with the story: Have you hesitated to respond to the call to love because you are too busy with distractions?

Do you seek only immediate gratification, lacking the patience to stay open to more difficult questions of life and love?

Are you upset that life has not progressed as you had anticipated? Are you angry that marriage is demanding more than you want to give? Do you resist the hard task of reprioritizing your lives?

The most difficult task for many married couples is to stay focused on a vision of love that sustains them through their desert time. Perhaps a small example from our own life will give you an idea of what we mean by refocusing.

After a candid discussion about the serious degeneration of a reflective atmosphere in our own household, we jointly reaffirmed a policy that we will not turn on the late news or watch late-night TV (unless there is a program of special interest). Our discussion yielded an awareness that the constant bombardment about what we lack (new cars, new looks, enticing food, new toys, new objects) creates unnecessary restlessness, and we don't need it.

The continued high-intensity assault to our senses became so irritating, we refused to subject ourselves to any more of it. More specifically, we refused to buy into the myth that the consumption of more goods will make us happy. We do not live by bread alone.

After staying the course for several weeks, we discovered a

real change in our marriage. Our deliberate screening out of unwanted and raucous noise fosters an environment that is quiet, peaceful and supportive of prayerfulness. Our home has once again turned into sacred space. It is easier to be around one another because we are more peaceful. The end of each day can now be reaffirmed as a time of rest and reflection on the meaning of our life.

We have also discovered that we are able to catch up on the world scene at other times during the day. We seem to have missed nothing.

What Do We Want to Say to God on the Basis of the Text?

That we cannot live by bread alone? That if we are to have a marriage that is reflective and deep, we must take the time to nurture it? That if *we* are not in charge of the interior atmosphere of our marriage, then who is?

Are we in the desert at the present time, with no familiar signposts or landmarks to help us find our way through it? Perhaps it is time to reset a few priorities and ask God to help us find a pathway through the desert.

What Difference Can This Text Make for How We Live Our Lives?

Get practical, and do an inventory of your lives. Who controls the atmosphere of your marriage? What could be rearranged, regulated, discarded or completely shut down to help foster an atmosphere that is more livable for you?

Decide on two (one for each of you) practical and concrete

changes that will improve the atmosphere of your marriage. Support one another as you implement them.

Lectio Divina:
Presumptions

Again, find your quiet space and listen to the word of God:

The devil then took him to the holy city and made him stand on the parapet of the Temple. "If you are the Son of God" he said "throw yourself down; for scripture says:

> "He will put you in his angels' charge,
> and they will support you on their hands
> in case you hurt your foot against a stone."

Jesus said to him, "Scripture also says:

> 'You must not put the Lord your God to the test.'"
>
> (Mt 4:5–7)

What Is the Text Saying in Itself?

This short section finds the tempter quoting the 91st Psalm, which promises God's unwavering protection in all matters. The nature of this temptation is traditionally defined as *presumption:* to live our lives with marginal responsibility for our choices and then assume that God will rescue us.

Jesus pulls the tempter up short by reminding him of the

mandate not to test God. He affirms the invitation to live life more fully, while not taking God's care lightly.

What Is God Saying to Us Personally?

Reflect on your life together: Where have you begun to balance out the obligations of marriage with a genuine confidence in God's care for you?

Have you been too presumptuous at times? Have you turned over the final responsibility for the emotional life of your marriage to your spouse? Because she is more comfortable with matters of the spirit, have you expected her to single-handedly foster the growth of the marriage?

Have you decided that you have gone far enough in your efforts to be open with one another? Does your presumption lead you to believe that your spouse will always be forgiving? Does this allow you to take advantage of her/his good will?

We suggest to couples that most marriages labor under the oppression of presumption. What couples demand from one another after two years of marriage would have been unheard of during their time of courtship. It leads to no end of grief and pain.

What Do We Want to Say to God on the Basis of the Text?

The scriptures reassure us that God, indeed, gives us the support and enlightenment we need to live a life of love. However, we cannot take God's love for granted. Nor can we take one another's love for granted.

Perhaps the most appropriate thing to say to one another is, "Let's be honest. Let's examine what we have done to one another under the weight of presumption. Let's confess to one another where we have grown resentful about unrealistic expectations in the marriage."

The confession of honesty in these matters teaches us that presumption is dealt with in two ways in a marriage. One way is to talk each day about the unfair burdens placed upon one another, then correct them with a new agenda of equality. Assumptions about who is responsible for what give way to a reworking of the responsibilities for our partnership.

The second way is to ask God for a clarity about where we are with one another. We suggest to couples that they pray for the kind of openness to one another that allows the compassionate God to touch them. Touched by God, they continue to grow in their capacity to build a marriage into a mutually satisfactory journey.

What Differences Can This Text Make for How We Live Our Lives?

Get practical once again. Sit quietly and catch your breath. Take a sheet of paper and write out what presumptions you see your partner making in your marriage. Describe in writing what a personal desert this has meant for you. Let your partner know what pain, anguish, uncertainty and loss of love these presumptions have created for you.

Read your descriptions to one another, pausing to hear not what you have done wrong, but what pain your partner endures because of your insensitivity. Construct a plan of action about correcting these presumptions and write out the plan. Be specific about what each of you will do. The more concrete the specific action, the more your plan will hold up.

Hold hands and ask God to help you find the strength you need to correct these matters. Now embrace one another in love. You have just entered more deeply into the hidden ground of love.

Lectio Divina: Grandiosity

Listen to the Word of God

Matthew continues:

> Next, taking him to a very high mountain, the devil showed him all the kingdoms of the world and their splendor. "I will give you all these" he said "if you fall at my feet and worship me." Then Jesus replied, "Be off, Satan! For scripture says:
>   'You must worship the Lord your God,
>   and serve him alone.'"
> Then the devil left him, and angels appeared and looked after him.
>
> (Mt 4:8–11)

What Is the Text Saying in Itself?

In the scriptures, the kingdoms of the world and all their splendor represent the outer world of superficiality, attraction

132

and deception. Jesus is invited to abandon his inner world in order to possess the entirety of the outer world. Yet he refuses, referring again to the Jewish ideal to serve God with a unified heart and with no promise of a good life. He opts for what we call *the downward mobility of a life of love.*

Jesus emerges from these trials as a lover of God, ready to enter into the heart of his ministry with a unified focus. Although most of us are not aware of the angels coming to minister to us as we pass through our own struggles, we can identify with the many pressures to live a life of comfort.

What Is God Saying to Us Personally?

The applications to marriage are simple. Here, too, the temptations to abandon the desire to love authentically can be numerous, and the results empty. Allow us to describe a real example of deep loss and genuine remorse.

"I think it was the affair that really did me in," said a friend one day. It is obvious he felt like talking, for the information flowed in an easy disclosure of all that had happened to him over several years.

"I had been married for fifteen years, and was really tired of the routine. My wife and I had completely lost touch with one another. I found myself coming to life over this woman in my office. She was alluring, very sensitive and listened to me. My feelings really came out, like I hadn't felt in twenty years.

"We stayed discreet for a time, then she started talking to me about how unhappy she was in her marriage. Once we went to bed together, we both became convinced that this relationship was made in heaven, and we pursued it full tilt."

He narrated that they seemed to do quite well at first by fighting common enemies. This bonded them together in a survival pact. Their partners found out about the affair, then their supervisor terminated both of them for violating company policy.

The tensions of two divorce actions at the same time confronted them harshly, yet they stayed the course because they believed in the power of their love. The more external forces tried to pry them apart, the more their determination to survive together galvanized. He now began to cry softly as he continued.

"We seemed to do just fine, as long as we couldn't have one another. The longing for permanence consumed us. Now that we have one another, it seems to be collapsing...have you ever awakened in the morning and known that you have been duped? I mean, that awful, sinking feeling in your stomach in knowing that your emotions, your mind, your thoughts played an awful trick on you? That you made the biggest mistake of your life?

"Do you know what this is like?" he repeats. "I mean it won't let go of me, and now I can't get it back. My kids hate me; they won't talk to me. I lost everything. It just slipped right through my fingers."

The consequences of this man's behavior will haunt him for the rest of his life. His wife no longer bothers to listen to him. Her own conflicts consume her. She carries a burning anger toward him, blaming him for the losses that stalk her.

The description of the temptations of Jesus end on a triumphant note. Stories of life like this one, find soothing angels nowhere in sight.

What Do We Want to Say to God on the Basis of the Text?

Perhaps it is time to ask God to help you face the grandiosity in your own life. Have you, like the man in the story above, been so badly blinded by a grandiosity about your personal competence that you made some horrible mistakes? Did it harm your marriage in a serious way?

We suggest to couples that God is always ready to open up a dialogue of love, but only if we are ready to face ourselves honestly. In fact, the greatest gift that we can bring to a marriage (and by that fact, to a relationship with God) is our honesty.

Perhaps it is time to acknowledge some real lessons about what you each did wrong, then ask God to assist you to deepen your love. This honesty is a direct entry into the hidden ground of love.

The Gospel presents the desert as a place of deep purification, and this purification often comes from seeing ourselves as we really are—when grandiosity collapses and we experience our poverty. Shared poverty and a deep prayerfulness bonds us at a soul level.

What Difference Can This Text Make for How We Live Our Lives?

Get practical once again and simply talk for a time. Share with one another where you see the grandiosity in one another's lives. Perhaps some of your stories are humorous. Try to laugh a bit, while you let the laughter soften your hearts. Make an agreement about what you need to change. Embrace one another and allow yourselves to feel the presence of God.

Into the Mystery of Love

In spite of our foibles, our faults and the efforts to love that end in pain, we interact with a God who loves us unconditionally. God invites us to enter into the heart of love, where God dwells.

In all, the quest for the personal God offers a sumptuous spirituality that leads to a rich and rewarding union with God and with one another. Couples slowly discover (both through their purification and their joy) that God becomes the substance of their love and the ground of their being.

Chapter 6: The Contemplative Marriage

The maturing of marriage over time can invite a couple to find their ground in the unfathomable dimensions of love. They begin to live with a comfortable and consistent intimacy with God—Love itself. Like the blossoming of a new flower, married love opens under the rays of the warm sun to present its unique gifts to the spouses who sincerely hunger for them. Thus, they enter into process four: *a contemplative marriage*.

Contemplation opens up a long, loving look at the beauty and simplicity of a marriage well lived. It invites the couple to stand in awe of the love that now permeates every dimension of their lives. They marvel at all that love means, how powerful it can be and how it gives texture and vitality to their life. They savor the many ways it renews their vision.

This kind of contemplation is open to any couple who works hard at making love the priority in their life. The sudden awareness of all that love is can overflow into tears of joy.

Those who know the unconditional love of God as the ground of everything they are, find another realization possesses them. They become aware that God is taking a more active role in their destiny. They evolve toward an open position to receive the gifts God continues to offer. They live in constant gratitude for God's generosity. Thus, every awareness related to their marital identity reflects a contemplative experience.

An Explanation

In our work with married couples, we tend to shy away from the word *contemplation* because it makes them feel uneasy. They may not be familiar with it or may believe it has nothing to do with the practicalities of daily married life. They associate the word with romantic sentiment or the stirring passion attached to new love.

Their doubts leave us in a dilemma about how to explain it, for the gift is a natural flowering of the Christian life, and married couples deserve to hear that contemplation is a legitimate dimension of their love.

The development of this rich gift brings with it the richest treasures of a marriage. That fact pushes us to find fresh ways to understand contemplation within a couple context. Allow us to begin our exploration with an illustration.

"I was standing at my kitchen window doing the dinner dishes while I watched my children playing with the neighbors' kids. I started to do the usual things, like worrying about what their futures might bring and praying for their safety. I was suddenly aware of the presence of God. My mind opened up. There was this feeling of unity—of OKness all of a sudden—and I just knew that they would be all right. Then I was flooded with peace. The awareness disappeared in a matter of a minute, but the peace remained as I continued watching them."

We consistently hear stories like this in our couple groups. Their occurrences remain mostly unspoken or unnamed because couples can be shy, yet the stories contain everything from a unitive experience like this one, to moving and very personal encounters with God.

We encourage couples to talk about rather than to flee from their experiences, to see them as expressions of God's love and then to name them. By orienting their reflections toward the word *contemplation*, we invite them to enter into a stream of tradition that not only legitimates their awakening, but fosters a new connection with God and with one another. It is an exercise in the awareness of something old and something new.

Some of them discover a deeper stratum in their love. Some finally name what they intuitively experience: God is alive and active in their hearts, and now they claim God's presence as the central experience of their marriage. They come home to the familiar ground of love that is God.

Our efforts at reorientation also connect them with the treasury of rich literature that has helped countless others understand the dynamics of their journey to God. Couples inherit this tradition just as readily as individuals, and they genuinely appreciate its contribution to their growth. In brief, we demystify the word *contemplation*.

Demystifying the Word

Frank X. Tuoti, spiritual writer and former student of Thomas Merton, in his refreshing work on the contemplative/mystical life, is clear about the magnitude of the task of demystification. He contends that the two words *contemplation* and *mysticism* are both poorly used and generally misunderstood. He calls them the most "bloodied" words in our language of the sacred.[28]

For that reason, we begin our work of demystification by

exploring the lived reality of married couples. We give them permission to tell their stories about their relationship with God. With a little coaxing, some sharing of our own and some reassurance that God loves them, they begin to tell us of the great work of God in their lives.

As their stories unfold we make an effort to work with a specific vocabulary in order to *name* their encounters. This effort helps extract these couples from the barnacled collection of misinterpretations, misunderstandings, distortions, biases, prejudices and fears associated with the word *contemplation.*

Suspiciousness toward the word flows from some negative assumptions that seem almost epidemic to married couples: that contemplation is the domain of professional religious or open only to the elite who are trained in theology. Some associate it with a celibate life or reserve it for those who have labored long and hard through the earlier stages of the spiritual life. Others restrict it to a monastic setting, seeing it as high ground reserved only for those who possess an exclusive calling.

Once we establish that God speaks a specific and very understandable language to married couples, the uncertainties about what they are dealing with seem to drop away. Their awareness opens to a realization that God speaks to them just as readily as to the more formally trained and vowed. The language, the imagery, the experiences are different but no less authentic. This awareness seems to open up their capacity to share more honestly, and their sharing flows from a plentiful reservoir of extensive connections with God.

Demystifying the term also removes it from some contemporary distortions that contribute to its bad name. Contemplation, for example, is not a series of glib "conversations with God," as if God were a good buddy who simply dictates the mystery of love in a rambling style that does little more than trivialize the sacred.

Neal Donald Walsch, in his book *Conversations With God,* reports that God dictates while Neal copies. His claims are received by many with great enthusiasm, pointing out that his works have turned their lives around. The claims are made because the hidden mystery of God suddenly becomes clear to them for the first time.

Although we don't doubt the sincerity of their efforts at enlightenment, God as ground of being, as transcendent mystery, as unfathomable Love, gets lost in the shadow of Walsch's vivid imagination. Walsch seems inclined to place himself in an exclusive position as the bearer of secrets. He seems to downplay everything but his own experience. His assertions take on a life that is bigger and more authentic than a disciplined study of the scriptures, commentaries by some very wise people, or an examination of serious and reasoned reflections by those who also seek God.

Another distortion is the equating of contemplation with paranormal, extranormal, or extraordinary events that "point" to God or "are" God. Some popular forms of spirituality insist that the extraordinary outweighs the ordinary, that the extreme is more believable than the common, and that God's most credible manifestation is in the outrageous, the bizarre, and the exceptional. God becomes an entertainer whose only mission in the cosmos is to make us "feel good."

We are sure that these manifestations are not a reflection of the genuine contemplative spirit, which seeks to find God in the ordinary, the routine, the now of life. Indeed, it finds God more in darkness than light, in emptiness rather than in good feelings, in the difficulties of married life rather than in the benign.

Nor is contemplation reserved for the unique few; it is for everyone. We assert that the key to appreciating this gift is in learning to take a different approach to prayer: to listen more and to speak less.

William Shannon correctly notes that the discovery of God is intimately connected to prayer. It is really an awakening to what the reality of life is. For him, two pillars support the development of contemplative spirituality. First, to understand that God is the Ground of all that is. Second, to become conscious, through prayer, of what is already there.[29]

As we evolve the discussion toward a definition of what their experiences mean, then introduce couples to the rich tradition associated with the contemplative gift, we help forge an important connection. They begin to understand that it is a gift for them, not one restricted to an elite core of professional religious. This helps them establish a new comfort with the word.

Thomas Merton himself questioned the entire supposition that makes contemplation or mystical prayer something strange and esoteric, reserved for a small class of almost unnatural beings. He believed the gift of infused contemplation is a generous gift of God that is offered to anyone who wants it or takes the time to pray for it.[30]

Going Live...Couples

We find ourselves again before a group of couples as we work to open up a notion of God's love as a contemplative experience. We give them permission to tell their stories, and they begin to come to life.

"We were praying silently one morning," begins a woman of about thirty-five. This is the first time she risks talking.

"It was the morning after a workshop we both attended on prayer and healing of memories. We sat close, each weighing our own thoughts silently, neither one of us sharing anything about the content of our prayers. It was clear from the quiet on both our parts that our prayer time was real. I broke the silence because I was curious about what he was feeling."

Her sincerity engages the group as the couples listen for familiar themes from their own lives. Her husband spontaneously joins the reflection.

"I was lifted out of my faltering efforts to pray by an image of God the Father," he says. "God was holding both of us on his lap in a tender embrace, utterly overjoyed with the fact that we love one another."

"I saw the same image," she continues, "...God holding us in an embrace of love, and so utterly pleased by our efforts. As the two of us talked a little later, we felt so close. We held each other and enjoyed this incredible love."

The couples remain silent for a time, measuring the intensity of their own love, or marveling at the wonder of this one. These and other stories help them experientially to demystify contemplation in marriage, and to identify it as a *lived and shared intuition of the presence of God*. They also help firm up our belief that God speaks to couples, often eloquently and dramatically, about the central place of love in their lives.

The stories echo John of the Cross's view that contemplation is "the infused loving knowledge of God." As Gregory the Great says, "It is a resting in God...the infused knowledge of God impregnated with love.[31]

"Above all," reiterates Thomas Merton, "it (contemplation) KNOWS the Source," even though this knowing can be obscure and unexplainable. Yet the degree of certitude this enlightenment brings with it takes it beyond the kind of knowing insured by intellectual certitude or simple faith.[32]

William Shannon, like Merton, describes the contemplative

experience as a discovery of an ultimate ground in which all contradictions, all opposites are united.[33]

We consistently hear couples speak of their experiences as unifying. They speak of the "righting" of their lives. They share a deepening internal unity. They trust their developing wholeness. They know that the contemplative experience grounds them in a free expression of the uniqueness of their persons.

This genuine KNOWING usually assumes a form that is personal to the couple itself. God speaks to them in a dramatic "breaking through" the limits of their lives. When they share, their love deepens through the gentle touch of God in their affirmation of one another.

"We were really in the midst of some very hard circumstances," states a middle-aged wife. Her face shows the strain of too many sleepless nights, too many burdens associated with family conflict.

"Our struggle had gone on for a long time, with things not going well for either one of us. Lots of conflict, lots of discomfort. Nothing seemed to go right for us. We turned once again to prayer, and that was labored, as it had been for months."

"Right...," her husband agrees. "It was awful; terribly empty for me. We were down to almost nothing in our checking account while the medical bills kept right on pouring in. The night we tried so hard to pray, I was about ready to give up."

"It opened up all of a sudden for us," she continues. "I...we both...had an image, an awareness, a rush or something, of God lifting us out of ourselves and bringing us together into the center of God, like into his very center, or heart, or being. The event was so powerful that it changed our life from thereon. We refer back to it frequently. There is no doubt, now, about God's care for us. We also worked our way through our problem."

This couple's encounter with God, like all descriptions of contemplation, sheds some light on its nature yet hardly exhausts the sacred dimensions of the experience. For every light that goes on in the contemplative experience, another shadow is cast. It is a real enlightenment, highly intuitive in its origin and fulfillment, yet somehow dark and obscure.

We listen intently as the couples reflect on the texture of light and dark in their lives:

"Clarity of some sort, yet still a darkness," says one. "We are still trying to figure out what it all means for us. We came out of it knowing that God will not solve our problems, but God remains faithful to us."

"A visitation from God; I know it was God. I just know it," states another.

"An awareness of God in every turn of our lives. A loving look at my beloved, my life, my kids, but ever so fleeting. It leaves me secure, but longing for more."

"It is God visiting us; we *know* it is God. Then it is gone and it's back to routine life, but we remain secure in knowing God is with us."

The contemplative moment (or microsecond) can vary significantly, even for a husband and wife within the same marriage. The sharing of the moment bonds them together in meaningful ways, while their very differences enrich its sharing. Consequently, God becomes more genuine and real through their interaction, each of them holding a unique insight into the meaning of God's love.

We suggest that the gift of contemplation is given to couples because God takes great delight in God's children loving one another. God's visitation confirms them in that love. God's embrace allows them to embrace one another. Like all contemplation, it is God who awakens them to a deeper love, and the awakening takes form around the different ways that spouses feel, know, intuit, sense, and conceptualize God. Thus, a great gift of the contemplative moment is a deeper bonding of the couple.

A Blending of Deeper Selves

An awakened I forms a deep bond with the awakened *You*. The I and the You meet in a deep exchange of love, and an awakened *We* comes to life. The invitation to journey into the hidden ground of love is accepted: by me, by you, by us. We grow: you, me and us as we make our choices, respond to the promptings of love in every life experience. We become different, yet our bond deepens through each interaction. I become more uniquely me and you affirm it. You become more uniquely you, and I support it. We become a deeply loving We, welcoming the shared experience of knowing the God of Love. God becomes the richest center of our bond.

Couples share the unfolding of their individual inner selves with each other. The movement toward the true self forms not only the ground of genuine contemplation, but the ground also firms up and takes on a specific definition through the evolution of intimacy. The fullness of what the couple seeks rests in God; its final fulfillment is in death.

As many spiritual writers insist, we cannot separate the true self of the person from the life of God. The true self is really God's life, manifested in the vitality and uniqueness of the individual person. Willigis Jäger, a contemporary spiritual writer, breaks his world into two convenient compartments as an expression of this reality. He notes that the true self is very simply God's life. Sinners are not aware that their life is really God's life, but saints live it to the fullest.[34]

Therefore, a healthy marriage within this context is more than just good communication, shared activities or enjoyable times together. Indeed, these features can be a gratifying dimension of a contemplative union, but they are not the final statement of what makes a contemplative marriage. Marriage is the reflection of two developing selves touched by God, blending together in a transforming union, seeking always to enter more seriously into the ground of love that is God. As God takes more and more initiative, the landscape of love becomes less a reflection of the couple's own desires and more of God's.

Some couples are called to make great sacrifices in the name of love. Contemplative love is never fixated on simply feeling good, for this kind of love calls a couple to penetrate in a more experiential way the mystery of love that is God.

This is not an easy journey, even though the call is issued to any couple who seeks the fullness of love. They are invited to die to their old images of what love is and to love more selflessly. Some are called upon to live a close connection to the suffering Christ through lives that are filled with pain and difficulty. They suffer greatly, yet find their bond deepens each day.

God embraces a couple's efforts to love with a special kind of care and concern for everything that happens to them. Consequently, one of the greatest gifts in their marriage is a special insight into the meaning of love and suffering.

Thomas Merton is very clear that the call to a contemplative life is not all consolation and fulfilling insight. He calls it "a terrible breaking and burning of idols."[35] He makes a strong case for the fact that contemplation invites a purification of self-serving mechanisms, false assumptions about self, life and God.

We suggest that any couple who has suffered through some of the hard lessons of the middle years of marriage, faced losses that are often a part of family life, or struggled to respond to the deep call of committed love, know a great deal about the breaking and burning of idols.

Unlike their monastic fellow travelers, they have a hard time naming their experiences. However, they somehow intuitively know that God is the deepest ground of their love.

"Every so often, sometimes at prayer, sometimes when we're tending to the family, I am caught up in the awesomeness of the whole thing," affirms one wife without hesitation. "I am suddenly aware of the goodness of this man, and how much he cares about me, us. It brings me to tears, and I have this need to share with him how grateful I am for his love."

"We are very close. We have come a long way together," states her husband wistfully. "At times I become aware of just how beautiful she really is, and how her beauty sustains me when I'm doubtful about myself. I am caught up in gratitude and really have a hard time expressing myself."

"I know we are brought together by God," begins an elderly couple. Their magnetism invites the younger couples to listen. "It has been clear from the first days of this marriage. We never had to work to feel a real union. We just know we are grounded in God, and the union we feel is based on that one great reality."

"I can't promise I will always love you perfectly," he says, "but I can be significant in bringing you to sainthood. I know I am sent into your life because this is where God wants me."

"I believe what you say," she answers. "I feel the same way. We can give one another no greater gift than to be loving and caring, and bring God to one another."

"We have always affirmed the value of a large family," says another. "The children have become our deepest joy. Our household is always intense, and we both have to work real hard to find space for genuine personal exchanges."

"She's so right," affirms her husband. "The dreams of a healthy, happy, vibrant family are so real. God is so present in the lives of our children. God speaks to us in the chaos and daily challenges of family living."

Contemplation in marriage carries a different flavor with it than in a monastic setting. God awakens awareness through the language of shared love, chaos of family activities, churnings about loyalty, dread about job instability, angst associated with deepening responsibilities, and a multiplicity of disjointed interactions that seem unrelated to anything sacred. Silence is a rare commodity.

The images associated with God's visitation may seem chaotic to an observer, but to the couple they are very sacred. God often speaks to them with the same endearing language with which they address one another. It is as if God becomes a part of the family madness: loving, reassuring, encouraging and supporting everyone.

Yet, true to the reality of contemplation, God's presence manifests itself in periodic surprises. This anchors a couple into an awareness of God's special faithfulness to them. The surprises usually come while they are wrestling with darkness. During these moments, they feel a *rightness* about their love for one another. They express an awareness of the unmistakable presence of God and they know it as deeply personal.

Most of the couples who speak of these matters have worked hard at finding a relationship with God. They know the fundamentals of prayer. They try to love one another genuinely, and listen for the voice of God in that love. The deeper

selves that awaken in contemplation reflect a genuine openness to receiving God's gifts. They understand that these gifts
cannot be coveted. They easily move to shared spontaneous
prayer as an expression that flows from these moments.

Watching and Waiting

In moving toward the second pillar of the contemplative
life (becoming aware of God, who is already there), couples
approach God with an expectant receptivity. They learn to be
quiet and listen for the voice of God, who calls them into
selfless love.

The marriage matures through an honest sharing of a
hunger for God, and the couple is bonded together at the
level of the transformed inner self. In brief, the couple willingly brings their entire life into an alignment that flows from
a sharing of two undivided hearts, and this action centers their
marriage in the heart of God.

Allow us to examine four ways in which a marriage reflects a
couple's deep hunger to make God the center of their life. Each
approach reflects a style of prayer that manifests a simple
expectancy: God is alive and visits us in our efforts to love well.

1. A simplification of life
2. Heartfelt attentiveness to God and to one another
3. An awareness of God's faithfulness
4. Waiting for God's visitation

We will not only explain the content of the four ways at
some length, but will also offer a brief *Lectio Divina* on each
of them.

Lectio Divina: Simplifying Life

Not so long ago, the two of us found ourselves unusually tense and short-tempered with one another. The tension came from a haunting realization that even though we live in a large, suburban, four-level split, we were running out of storage space. The crowding was getting to us, so we expressed our reaction to it through great impatience.

We are generally wise shoppers, but after twenty-four years of marriage, we found our house bursting at the seams. Even though we periodically purge the house of objects that are out-of-date or no longer essential, we needed to do something. Our animated discussion about what to do finally led us to select one choice from four options:

1. Move into a bigger house;
2. Build more storage space (and fit our middle-aged bodies into less living room);
3. Rent one of those free-standing storage units now popping up all over town;
4. Forget the rationalizing, admit that middle age is upon us and simplify life by downsizing.

After an honest exchange about what we really need to sustain our life, we decided to downsize and simplify.

We began sorting through a collection of old Christmas

decorations, out-of-date clothes, worn carpets, stained plastic yard furniture and an endless array of decorator items that were once a priority. After an entire day of yeas and nays about which objects were to live and which would die, we delivered the still useful objects to someone who accepted them graciously as real treasures.

Several weeks later, we saw the last vestiges of our pack-rat predilections hauled off to their new home, and we embraced one another with a sigh of relief. We had now achieved a distinctly American middle-class kind of freedom, for no people on the face of the earth have ever possessed so many material goods while still longing for more. We felt free because we had opted for a simpler vision of what marriage means.

If the gospel writers were to observe the large number of possessions that Americans see as essential for survival, they would probably have pushed more vociferously for the simplified life. Jesus, in. Matthew's Gospel, offers this straightforward mandate to anyone who joins the ranks of discipleship:

Listen to the Word of God

"Cure the sick, raise the dead, cleanse the lepers, cast out devils. You received without charge, give without charge. Provide yourselves with no gold or silver, not even with a few coppers for your purses, with no haversack for the journey or spare tunic or footwear or a staff, for the workman deserves his keep. Whatever town or village you go into, ask for someone trustworthy and stay with him until you leave."

(Mt 10:8–11)

What Is the Text Saying in Itself?

Jesus presents a brief instruction to his twelve closest followers on simplicity of spirit. Note, however, that a simplified lifestyle is not an end in itself. It is intimately linked to service. The power to heal, which emanates from God, is freed to flow more readily through a lifestyle that encourages a disciple to stay mobile. Discipleship is equated with a trust in the care of God, who will provide for all that is needed.

What Is God Saying to Us Personally?

Share the above text in a reflective way with your spouse. It can be readily applied to marriage, for the same call goes forth to those couples who desire to share their discipleship.

The Gospels invite us to be countercultural: to share a life of simplicity and trust in God's care. The culture of consumerism relentlessly seduces us into a glitzy victimhood. We measure the quality of life by how much we possess. We value the person by how much they earn or the magnitude of their net worth.

The Gospels invite us to simplify life in order to spend more of our energy doing the work of love. Loving one another, finding God as the ground of love, invites us to seek simplicity in all matters.

What Do We Want to Say to God on the Basis of the Text?

The first response is to be more conscious of what God is asking of us. Live simply. Trust God. This is the spirit of the contemplative call. We are asked to reform our lives, not to

make them difficult, but to create the needed space to discover the God who is already there.

Take these questions, and reflect on them:

1. Where does attachment to material things cloud your
   image of love? What possessions actually get in the way
   of knowing God as the ground of your love?
2. What is the restlessness you feel that never seems to
   leave, even after new purchases? Is this very restlessness
   inviting you to reevaluate? To be less busy? Less distracted?
3. Are you too involved in too many activities to open up a
   life of genuine sharing? Is God inviting you to change
   your lifestyle?

Chronic busyness is a common American illness. Our
minds can be as cluttered as our closets, never allowing us to
hear or feel the presence of God. Listen to the testimony of
this couple and see if their experiences are not like your own:

"We spent far too many years climbing the social ladder,"
she says. "It took a serious illness for me to get my priorities
straight. I was flat on my back and had nothing to do but
search for some kind of meaning to all this pain. I clearly
heard the voice of God speak to me and tell me to get a focus
for my life: 'I love you too much to allow you to miss the purpose of your existence.' That really shook up my priorities,
and we have finally gained a marriage."

What Differences Can This Text Make for How We Live Our Lives?

Decide on a concrete plan of action to simplify your life.
Create the open space your marriage needs to recover the

hidden ground of love. Think of this concrete action as an effort to open up a healing mode within your marriage. God's success in reaching us is related to an internal atmosphere that is uncluttered, open, spacious and loving.

Lectio Divina: Heartfelt Attentiveness to God and to One Another

The ordinary becomes extraordinary in marriage because God lives in every event, each interaction, every effort to make love more genuine.

The practical task for a couple is to listen for the voice of God in their interaction. Heartfelt attentiveness comes through clearly in this example.

"I was after him all the time to respond to me," she says. "He never satisfied my needs. I was very unhappy because he never gave me what I desire. In the midst of a great intensity one day, it suddenly came to me that if I want him to hear me, I must also give him an honest hearing. That realization opened up something, and we have learned to be more respectful to one another. We can listen now, because we realize our success has a lot to do with knowing that God really does live in our marriage."

We often call this style of attentiveness to a spouse *the art of contemplative listening*. It flows from an awareness that God dwells in the deepest center of a relationship. Respect for one another's processes is its most direct expression. Spouses listen to one another because God's love invites them to be open to the living presence of God within the marriage.

We invite you to once again look to an image of love from St. John's Gospel.

Listen to the Word of God

"I am the true vine,
and my Father is the vinedresser.
Every branch in me that bears no fruit
he cuts away,
and every branch that does bear fruit he prunes
to make it bear even more.
You are pruned already,
by means of the word that I have spoken to you.
Make your home in me, as I make mine in you.
As a branch cannot bear fruit all by itself,
but must remain a part of the vine,
neither can you unless you remain in me.
I am the vine,
you are the branches.
Whoever remains in me, with me in him,
bears fruit in plenty;
for cut off from me you can do nothing."

(Jn 15:1–8)

What Is the Text Saying in Itself?

The imagery is straightforward, for Jesus makes a strong statement about the intricate and unbreakable connection between God's love and our own lives. With God we can do all things. Without God, we can do nothing. It is as if the blood of God flows through our veins.

What Is God Saying to Us Personally?

The heart of a contemplative marriage beats with the pulse of God. Read the text on the interplay between the vine and branches once again, then see if you can find the presence of God in your own marital experience:

1. How does your marriage speak of the real connection between the life of God and your own? Has your marriage yielded fruit, or have you cut yourselves off from the life of God by indifference or laziness?
2. Can you open your eyes more widely to see the presence of God in your sincere efforts to love?
3. Pruning can be a painful process, yet God prunes in order to create new life and to help us bear more fruit. Are there areas in your life where God is now pruning? What do you make of it? If you were the vine dresser on your own behalf, in which areas of your life would you prune away the dead branches?

What Do We Want to Say to God on the Basis of the Text?

The message of the text is a simple one: We are intimately connected to the life of God. We depend upon God for everything, whether or not we are ready to recognize that fact. Apart from God we can do nothing. Those who live the life of God inevitably bear fruit as a reflection of their deep connection with God.

These realities comprise the most basic position in the contemplative life. Some refer to this reality as our fundamental poverty before God.

Share several ways you have become more aware of God's goodness on your behalf.

Share several ways that an awareness of the dependency on God has changed your life.

Share the ways this will influence the vision of what your marriage can be.

What Difference Can This Text Make for How We Live Our Lives?

Draw up a new time schedule for yourselves, making some more room to spend time together with God. In the scripture reading, Jesus speaks about "abiding with me." Do some real pruning of your lives by deciding how you might abide with God. If you are like most couples, you can find plenty of room to prune away the activities that have no lasting value.

We discovered, for example, that creating a quiet space in the morning or shutting off late-night TV gave us a large portion of time to nurture our souls, and it yields much fruit.

For most of us, God does not ask for great sacrifices or heroic virtue. God asks, instead, that we use our gifts well and that we slowly turn our hearts toward a genuine dwelling with God. Once on track with the joys of spending time with God, couples find that this time period becomes the most enjoyable part of the day. Letting go of distractions, frivolities or meaningless activities is welcome because it opens up the way to an awareness of God in all things.

Dwelling with God can be as simple as reading the scriptures together, then sitting quietly as the lessons lock in.

Sharing distinctly feminine and masculine views of the stories enables both spouses to stretch and grow.

These actions are not the gift of contemplation as such. They are necessary efforts to open up a life of prayer. However, many of our couples state that within this context, God is most dynamic in their lives. God speaks with love and tenderness in the silent gaps in the relationship or in the soul sharing that follows. These are often the richest of contemplative moments.

Now decide what steps you will take to dwell with God.

Lectio Divina:
An Awareness of God's Faithfulness

In one of our previous books, *The Soul of a Marriage,* we took Psalm 90, which we say together almost every morning, and reframed it for couples. It is an ancient song of praise to a faithful God, but we rewrote it in a way that reflects our conviction of God's loyalty to us. We still turn to this song of praise when we feel the need for a creative expression or when we want to remember God's goodness to us.

Periodically, we renew our creativity by rewriting the psalm in such a way that it expresses our current state of awareness of God's presence. We generally rediscover one or more of the consistent themes about God's faithfulness that have been there from the beginning of our marriage. We also get in touch with the freshness of the now of life under God's care.

Each of the psalms invites a creative response of this sort. They are public prayers, so we are free to personalize them. They invite us to make the powerful sentiments a part of our experience. With a personal nuancing, they can express a deep part of us in ways that traditional language cannot express.

We encourage married couples to try this same technique of praying intimately. Listen for echoes of your own experiences with God as you read this prayer.

Listen to the Word of God

Variations on Psalm 90

Our long days together collapse
into a blurred passage of waking dreams.
Obligation and sameness, one day upon another;
yet, in Your awareness, they remain a timeless imprint
of Love upon love.

The days slowly unfold
under the gentle press of Your care.
Nothing goes unnoticed.
All remains fresh; life renews.

Our struggles to come to wisdom,
marked by little else than honest efforts to know,
to sustain a clear vision,
bring us event by event into the Center of Love,
where we meet You with our gifted consciousness.

Restless moments in the night,
talking light while we confront the darkness,
seeking refuge in the womb of compassion,
bring peaceful sleep under Your watchful care.

What treasures you lavish upon us, Creator God.
How many years left?
How many more days of feeling your healing power cross
the chasm between us and those whom you send?
What more will you expect from us?

The shortness of our growing time,
the efforts to come to maturity,
the reminders of our still-nagging frailties and fears,
bring wisdom of heart.

How many more left, and how rich will they be?
Tell us: what is the sequence of days with,
and without one another?
Give us a vision we can trust.

We stand in awe of what You have done.
We wait with patient expectancy because you desire more.
We remain loyal to our call,
and ask that this awareness remain
when our too-human days rob us of care,
and deepen our impatience with one another.

May your love sustain us always,
and the work of our hands be brought to fullness.

What Is the Text Saying in Itself?

It clearly is a song of gratitude for the God who is faithful,
and this faithfulness is larger than our awareness of the day-to-
day events of our brief histories. We reflect on the generosity
of God in every happening, each urge, each vision of our lives.

Within this context, even the events that seem like failure at
the time of their occurrence are somehow redeemed by God's

love. We ask that God help us see what cannot readily be seen. We ask that this vision of God sustains us.

The prayer is essentially optimistic, for this God of love will be there for us for the duration of our histories. We do our best to remain open to the continued love of God in the coming events of life and ask that God's work with us be brought to fullness.

What Is God Saying to Us Personally?

Marriage is more than just a stretch of history in which we create a life together. It carries eternal significance. Living a life of deep love offers glimpses of a total experience of love that will be grounded in God for all eternity.

What Do We Want to Say to God on the Basis of the Text?

Perhaps it is time to identify with the sense of continuity that the psalm conveys. Perhaps it will help you see that God is loyal and that this loyalty is a reflection of God's eternal design.

Maybe it is a matter of simply reading the psalm to one another as a shared prayer, then sitting in silence while the divine lesson touches each of you.

Perhaps this is the prayer that will help each of you learn to pray from your heart. It gives you permission to read a new spirit into an ancient prayer. It is a genuine blending of something old and something new. Allow your inner selves to express your sentiments and open yourselves up to prayer.

What Differences Can This Text Make for How We Live Our Lives?

Get practical by taking some cues from our variations on Psalm 90. Take this psalm (or another that you both like) and rewrite it as an expression of the love in your marriage.

You can do it individually by selecting a psalm that speaks most clearly to you; then share your artistry with your beloved.

You can work jointly on a creative rewrite, talking together as you construct the language of prayer. The joint action is an engaging exercise of love in itself. It can open up a new experience of the presence of God in your sharing.

Lectio Divina: Waiting for God's Visitation

Couples who learn to live patiently while waiting for God's visitation are much less intense about making their relationship perfect. They approach marriage on a much different basis than the couples who strive for a more sensitive interaction. Indeed, they become very sensitive, but the sensitivity flows from an openness to God's healing presence in the marriage.

They live with a beautiful trust that God is with them. They support one another during dark times. They share a peacefulness that is grounded in God's love. They know that God will bring forth rich gifts at the proper time. They trust more in God's timetable than in their own.

More than any other awareness, these couples know that every event in their lives somehow invites them into a deeper relationship with God.

Psalm 131 is a simple song. It is brief, to the point and contagious in its spirit, for it speaks to the reader about waiting patiently for the visitation of God. Pause a while; quiet your soul.

Listen to the Word of God

Yahweh, my heart has no false pride;
my eyes do not look too high.
I am not concerned with great affairs
or things far above me.
It is enough for me to keep my soul
still and quiet
like a child in its mother's arms,
as content as a child that has been weaned.
Israel, hope in Yahweh,
now and for always!

(Ps 131)

What Is the Text Saying in Itself?

The simple, straightforward imagery of the song invites us to quiet down and wait for God. Although the psalm can be interpreted as a national lament during a time of serious political turmoil, it can be easily interpreted in a personal way.

The image of a child quiet and at rest in its mother's arms conveys comfort and security. Its impact upon the reader is immediate, for we are invited to rest with confidence and peace. This God can be trusted. This God is not only the ground of love, but the foundation for hope.

The inner state of resting, watching, waiting and hoping for the visitation of God not only brings about a tranquil state, it also invites a change of life. Simplicity, stepping aside from the turmoil of the great affairs in life, or an effort to live simply creates a heart that is open to receiving the heart of love.

What Is God Saying to Us Personally?

In marriages that are deep and real, we find a great peacefulness. The spouses literally know they can trust the God who dwells with them. They set aside time each day to quiet down, be at peace, and await the visitation of God. They know that it is God who is loving them into a wholeness, and they are grateful for God's gifts. Their gratitude sometimes gives them the innocence of a child in its mother's arms.

Even though couples continually remind us that they are impossibly busy, we assure them that God blesses their every effort to create a solid family life. Patient expectancy helps ground them in an awareness that God speaks to them differently than to couples who have the free time to nurture their souls through solitude.

We remind them that God will respond to their efforts to love with a continued outpouring of spiritual gifts. To make the gifts a more conscious discovery, we sometimes use the phrase of the English spiritual writer, Evelyn Underhill. She speaks of "the sacrament of the present moment."[36]

She affirms that God visits the person with special gifts, no matter how busy their life. God is there in all the sights and sounds, joys, pains and sacrifices of life. As we suggest to couples, patient expectancy implies learning to listen, feel and discover the presence of God in the simplest matter.

What Do We Want to Say to God on the Basis of the Text?

God honors all our efforts, no matter how small or time-limited. Ask God to help you foster an awareness that each moment is a gift. Each moment is a potential contemplative experience.

What Difference Can This Text Make for How We Live Our Lives?

Do a very simple task: Decide what events in your marriage speak to you most clearly about God's love. Is it dealing with your children? Is it sharing your sexuality? Is it bonding with one another over new projects? Decide how you can slow down the momentum of life just enough to see the presence of God in these events. Decide on a practical plan, then make an effort to implement it each day.

Living a Contemplative Marriage

Our view of contemplation places God at the deepest center of a marriage. This experience invites a couple to become aware of the unmistakable dynamic of God's love at work in every interaction, each shared encounter, each ordinary event of their life, every dream of the future. A deep union evolves as a couple learns to KNOW God as the source of their reality.

At times, their knowing is disconcertingly dark and obscure; at other times it is amazingly clear and focused. Both modes of knowing are manifestations of the presence of the living God.

These deepening, and all-too-frequently unnamed experiences slowly evolve toward a dimension of marriage that is grounded and sheltered in the mystery of God's love. Sharing their awarenesses of this mystery, unites two separate selves in a union that transcends the practical intimacy attained solely on personal initiatives.

Couples who arrive in this place have generally paid a heavy price for their gifts. They have struggled with making marriage work. They have learned to communicate. They have been through trial and suffering, and have determined not to be beaten by marital strife and uncertainty.

They know each other's persons, complete with strengths and shortcomings, and they have learned to love one another deeply. Thus, sensitivity, genuine honesty and pervasive gratitude characterize their marriage.

They thrive on the daily practice of individual and shared prayer. It is during these moments that they feel most at home with God. This helps them carry the presence of God within them wherever they go.

Their relationship with God is moving and personal. They daily weigh their intimacy with God and speak openly of their destiny. Their process carries them beyond themselves to a developed sense of justice and a contagious form of compassion.

In a contemplative marriage the couples generally maintain the delicate balance among the three selves, and do it with ease. They respect one another because they see all interaction as an expression of God's work in their lives.

They enjoy a special gift of peace because they realize that God is taking more and more initiative for their future. This awareness gives their love the same quality of patience, unconditionality, and tenderness with which God loves them.

Interestingly, those around them know they have achieved a

successful marriage, and their peacefulness and confidence give them a *presence* that makes others curious. They are often asked the question, "How do you explain your success in marriage?" They find it difficult to be dogmatic about where their success comes from, preferring instead to be quiet about the intricacies of their relationship and their connection with God.

They live in a time of expectancy, firmly believing that God will bring their lives to fulfillment. The fulfillment of this sort of marriage is expressed, again, through the image of a tent:

> For we know that when the tent that we live in on earth is folded up, there is a house built by God for us, an everlasting home not made by human hands, in the heavens....This is the purpose for which God made us, and He has given us the pledge of the Spirit.
>
> (2 Cor 5:1, 5)

This is a unique process of marital spirituality enjoyed in its fullness by relatively few couples. Moreover, there seems to be little information available about its dynamics. Couples have a difficult time finding a direction or counsel as their spirituality matures, so they often live with puzzling dark nights about the validity of their experiences.

They even find themselves isolated at times in a special kind of uncertainty. They search diligently to find couple friends who share their views but have little luck.

Their dark nights can actually deepen as they respond to the call to spend more time in reflection. This removes them from interaction with couples whose lives are often busy and frivolous.

The few couples we know who live this process have arrived at it through a trust in God that their destiny is in God's hands and that God will never abandon them. They live with great confidence and peace.

Chapter 7:
Enhancing Wholeness

We hope that by this time, you have learned a great deal about the hidden ground of love and how it forms the foundation for a vital marital spirituality. We also trust that you now have a better idea about how growth in marital spirituality leads to a genuine wholeness, both personally and within the marriage relationship.

In the first chapter, we placed the term *wholeness* at the center of our explorations and suggested that living a dynamic life of love always fosters it. Union with God is its final integration. The popular adage "holiness is wholeness" expresses this reality most clearly. The spiritual writer Willigis Jäger nuances the close connection between these dimensions by noting that *healthy* and *holy* are words derived from the same root.[37]

In order to explore the quest for wholeness in greater detail, allow us to return to the three methods of growth in marital spirituality described in our earlier chapters:

Quieting Down
Lectio Divina
Marital Process

We will briefly reexamine each of these dimensions and invite you to apply them in imaginative ways to re-create your marriage. Think of this new effort as variations on a theme, inviting you to achieve a wholeness that is unique for your life context.

We make no attempt to present specific methodologies for growth in their complete forms. If you choose, you can explore these methods more seriously by reading the works of the authors included in these pages.

Variations on a Theme:
Quieting Down: Breathing

Physician Andrew Weil develops an extensive exposition of the role of breathing in fostering wholeness, holiness and health by speaking of breath as the movement of the spirit. He believes that the breath connects the person to all of creation. Consequently, his simple exercises in breathing become a form of spiritual practice.[38]

In one of his exercises entitled *let yourself be breathed,* he invites his readers to imagine themselves evolving into a living part of a wider universe, while the dynamic cosmos actually breathes for them. Thus, breathing forms an organic connection with all of reality. It forms a cosmic consciousness.

Weil's cosmic connections seem to be very close to what we mean by an experience of the sacred. No matter how expansive his explanation of what simple breathing brings with it, his method can be useful for quieting down and thereby developing an openness of spirit. He gives specific instructions on how many breaths to take.[39]

Quieting Down: Prayer of Awareness

William Shannon suggests an exercise in wordless prayer as a pathway to quieting down. In what he calls a *prayer of awareness*, he invites his readers to take some time away from the routine of life and to move inward. He recommends drawing in a few simple breaths, followed by a phrase like "help me to live in Your presence."

He then suggests his readers breathe out while letting go of their cares and concerns, pointing out that "letting go" of these distractions invites an awareness of the presence of God. If we become distracted, Shannon suggests we not become tense or preoccupied with clearing the mind, but simply redirect our thoughts back toward an awareness of God. He also suggests that after a period of time, practitioners of his method conclude with the Lord's Prayer or a favorite psalm.[40]

We often refer to this state of quiet as a *conscious grounding in love*. Through the consistent use of any solid method of quieting down like this one, a practitioner cannot help but discover a new wholeness and communicate that same wholeness to others.

Quieting Down: Merton's Own Method

Thomas Merton, encouraged by many who knew him, recorded his method for quieting down in one of his journals. This description found its way to one of his friends in a personal letter written in 1966. His method seems deceptively simple, yet it must be remembered that he lived in a monastic setting and practiced various prayer forms for twenty-five years before he recorded his method.

His technique is that of culling from his mind anything that dampens the experience of the sacred, thereby freeing him to place total attention on the presence of God. He describes a kind of praise that rises spontaneously from his heart. His prayer progresses under its own momentum until he describes himself as becoming lost in the presence of God.[41]

Merton is not easy to understand, even though he is widely acknowledged as a master of the spiritual life. His description leaves a reader with more questions than answers about the specifics of this technique. However, he is not advocating a technique as such. He is simply answering a request to explain what he does when he prays. In brief, he describes a simple method of prayer rather than a technique of quieting down, even though the end results are the same.

Some of Merton's critics claim he is too complicated to emulate, but we find couples who report that a simple, prayerful connection with God works well for them. They quiet down quickly, enter into the ground of love with a pure heart and remain there. They believe that more structured methods of prayer are cumbersome. We assure them a sound rule of spiritual growth applies to them: "simpler is better."

Quieting Down: Timeless Healing

Herbert Benson, M.D., links health of mind, body and spirit to what he calls "the relaxation response."

The relaxation response is simple in form, for it is composed of two basic steps: First, slowly repeat a word (or phrase or sound or prayer). Second, keep the mind uncluttered by thinking of nothing in particular. If common, everyday thoughts intrude into consciousness, it is best to passively disregard them. This allows the user to return to the repetition of a phrase.[42]

This two-step method is about as close as he gets to a formal method of quieting down. He disavows a specific, formal technique and asserts that the relaxation response can be evoked in a large number of ways, such as meditation, prayer, autogenic training, progressive muscle relaxation, jogging, swimming, Lamaze breathing exercises, yoga, tai chi chuan, chi gong or even knitting and crocheting.[43]

To facilitate "quieting," he suggests that practitioners try one of these focus words: *one, ocean, love, peace, calm, relax.* He also suggests prayers for those who quiet down through an awareness of the sacred. He offers a selection of prayer phrases that suit the needs of most practitioners:

Christian (Protestant or Catholic):
  "Our Father who art in heaven"
  "The Lord is my shepherd"
Catholic:
  "Hail Mary, full of grace"
  "Lord Jesus Christ, have mercy on me"
Jewish:
  "Sh'ma Yisroel"
  "Shalom"
  "Echod"
  "The Lord is my shepherd"
Islamic:
  "Insha'allah"
Hindu:
  "Om"

He encourages his readers to practice his quieting method twice a day for ten or twenty minutes.

Quieting Down: Centering Prayer

Trappist monk Thomas Keating has developed a clearly defined method to engage his students in what he calls a "centering prayer." His method begins with a view of God that posits God as active in our lives, since God invites every person into a contemplative relationship. Our task is simply to quiet down and prepare ourselves for the encounter with God.

Keating offers four simple steps. He invites his readers to choose a sacred word as a symbol of their desire to respond to God's presence within them (e.g., "Abba," "Jesus," "Come, Lord Jesus," "Peace"). Then he invites his practitioners to sit comfortably with their eyes closed, settle briefly, then repeat the sacred word slowly and reverently within themselves.

If they become aware of distractions, he invites them to firmly but gently refocus on the repetition of their sacred word. At the end of a twenty-minute prayer period, he invites them to remain in silence with their eyes closed for a couple of minutes.[44]

Breathing: Buddhism

By now it should be clear that even though these contemporary mentors represent different disciplines, their methods of quieting down have a great deal in common. The single unifying thread in each of their methods is the emphasis on slow breathing.

The Buddhist author Thich Nhat Hanh reminds us that our breath is actually the bridge between body and mind. Breath reconciles the actions of the body with the presence of the mind. It aligns diverse parts of us. It illuminates. It brings peace and calm.[45]

Addressing Some Practicalities

Couples are often puzzled about how these methods of quieting down (which are for individuals) work to enhance a developing marital spirituality. We suggest to them that any methodology needs to be creatively adapted to the marital experience, so we recommend one or more of the following ways to foster a sharing of quiet time:

1. Seeking and finding quiet space during the day centers you in your own truth, and that brings wholeness. The wholeness you radiate helps make your spouse whole. Thus, any personal effort to stay centered is indirectly shared in a close relationship and benefits both partners.

2. Staying in the same room while you both quiet down, even if you utilize different methods, is a real sharing of quiet. The flow of positive energy from one person to another makes quieting down contagious. It can anchor you both in a feeling of wholeness.

3. Before falling asleep at the end of the day, try breathing quietly side by side for fifteen minutes. When you have found a composed center within each of you, embrace one another and allow your bond to deepen.

4. Quiet down using separate spaces and different techniques. Afterward, dialogue about your lives. It opens up the vast and unexplored potential of love.

5. Get creative and try some different methods of quieting down. Share with one another what works and what doesn't. In this way you can become good teachers to one another. Keep searching until you find a method that is appropriate for your needs as a couple.

6. Be generous. Perhaps the greatest gift you can give to each other is to spell off one another from the continual

pressures of family obligations. In this way, you can help your spouse claim some quiet space. Their quieting down will contribute to the wholeness you both seek.

Variations on a Theme:
Lectio Divina

We also hope, by this time, that you understand more about *Lectio Divina* as a method of growth. We have slowly evolved our own process into one that is so vital, we cannot live without it.

Our first encounters with the scriptures were characterized by hesitance and lack of direction, so we reached for several off-the-shelf commentaries to help us understand the texts themselves. The *New Jerome Biblical Commentary*, published by Prentice-Hall, is especially helpful. It is always within our reach and has proven itself to be indispensable for helping us uncover the rich layers of meaning present in the scriptures.

Taking time to study the origins, historical background, literary forms and intent of the authors not only facilities a deeper understanding of the word of God, but enriches our sharing as well. Over time, we have gained a great deal of knowledge about what it means to be formed by the power of God's word.

As we evolved, we discovered specific texts that speak to us in a special way. We often return to several psalms, for example, and have actually memorized them. We recall them during the day or repeat them during times of crisis.

We have also read our way through several books of the Bible, sometimes a phrase at a time. This slow, delicious savoring of a good story gives us a feeling for the continuity of the text. It also fosters an appreciation for the storytelling capacity of an evangelist like Luke, who uses all the techniques of a good novel writer to lead us to a relationship with the compassionate God. Dante described Luke's artistry as *"Scriba Mansuetudinis Christi"* ("the recorder of Christ's loving kindness").[46]

We evolved over time into more creative modes, because *Lectio Divina* is a progressive dialogue with God, and God engages us at different levels. Generally, we move toward the deeper ground of love. We always walk away enlightened. We usually gain direction and strength when we ask for it. In all, *Lectio Divina* is the most important training we receive in the art of loving God and one another.

The progress has been slow and certain, with each insight into the reality of God's love yielding specific rewards. Perhaps the slow certainty of its evolution is why Michael Casey describes growth in *Lectio Divina* as "a lifelong process of turning toward God."[47] It is not the realm of the quick-fix, feel-good spirituality, or new-age gimmickry. He compares this learning process to a "marathon" rather than a "sprint."[48]

He advises that it is better to spend five minutes a day and do *Lectio Divina* well, rather than to focus on long encounters with the scriptures, then quit because of fatigue, lack of time or boredom.[49] As we discovered in some of our early efforts, brief periods with shorter readings yield great satisfaction. Sometimes a simple phrase becomes the core of a rich experience.

We have discovered, as you will, that confidence grows over time. As with athletic training, it is better to start slowly, then run longer distances as strength increases. Confidence allows us to exercise variations in the ways we proceed. Allow us to share a few of our experiences:

1. *Vocalizing* the text slows a person down. It forces readers to dwell on the content, context and specific nuances of the words.[50]

We vary our pace from day to day. After our initial quieting down using a method of breathing, one of us will take the lead and read a section of text. We sometimes remind one another to slow down or to reread the text several times over. This maintains a sacred feel for what we hear. It might take three or more readings to finally get the gist of what the author is trying to convey. It might take several more repetitions to move toward a quality reflection. So be it, for there is no hurry.

It is important to remember that just because we accept the scriptures as the living word of God, we are still dealing with human text, and it can be very hard to understand. When in doubt, rather than guessing, we consult a reliable scholarly commentary.

Choice of a text for the day varies. If we are reading our way through a specific book, we continue on from where we left off the day before. We might read only a brief paragraph further before calling each other into silence and reflection, followed by dialogue. We let God take the lead and enlighten us as God wills. Sometimes a new insight is quick and surprising. Sometimes insights flow only after a period of hard work.

We vary the context at times with seasonal readings by following the outline for the yearly liturgical cycle. Guidebooks are readily available in church pews or can be purchased through a liturgical publishing house.

Which one of us reads on a particular day is arbitrary. If one of us likes a specific text, the choice is an easy one. Dialogue and prayer usually flow spontaneously from the text. If a text ends in prolonged quiet, that is quite acceptable, for we have learned that God's word works subtly. Sometimes the most appropriate response is a simple, respectful silence. Sometimes we share the results of the silence, sometimes not. The critical matter in our growth is respect for one another's processes. As any married couple knows, processes vary significantly from day to day, so the *Lectio* blends in with a prevailing atmosphere in the marriage.

2. *A vocalized text has more impact.* If you have ever read the scriptures in a liturgy or at a public gathering, you know that hearing yourself read aloud can create an entirely new meaning for the text.

You know you have to work a bit harder to pronounce difficult words, or slow down to develop a specific meaning to a phrase, or be clear about what the text is conveying.

Reading aloud within a marital context might even be more difficult, since spouses know each other too well. The scriptures push and prompt us to examine our lives at a root level, and spouses can be quick to infer what needs to be changed in the other (rather than themselves). Yet the scriptures consistently call us back to see the truth of our motivations.

If the text invites us to be merciful, we cannot help but examine ourselves and our willingness to forgive. Reading out loud also pushes the reader to be responsible to the relationship. Spouses cannot sidestep the obvious. The reading can end in silence because the truth speaks for itself.

Reading can sometimes end in shared laughter because a couple is poignantly reminded of their foibles. Some of the moments of great insight for any couple flow from a hearty laugh. God is present there just as readily as in heart-rending disclosures.

3. *Vocalizing the text is a means of avoiding distractions.* It is practically an impossible task, contends Michael Casey, to read a scripture text out loud while allowing one's mind to wander somewhere else.[51] We concur. The act of vocalizing gives the text an enormous weight. It is like an imprinting in our minds that lasts for an entire day.

This deliberate attention to the scriptures often opens a spontaneous dialogue that stimulates us to be reflective for the rest of the day. We then reference events of the day back to the original text, thereby deepening the meaning of the scriptures.

Variations on a Theme:
Marital Process

We have consistently discovered that *Lectio Divina* opens up an awareness of the presence of God in all things. As we have become more familiar with the many ways that God speaks to us through its practice, we have gained confidence in its capacity to help us find our way through life. We do not hesitate to be creative in its use, because we take our cues from the monastic experience: do not be afraid to experiment.[52]

When we get creative, *Lectio Divina* takes on any number of specific complexions. It is challenging to the ways we experience God. It is supportive in our endeavors to grow. It is a wide and clear window into the hidden ground of love. It stimulates, affirms and deepens our views. It brings encounters with the living God, and they enhance our understanding of what it means to live passionately. It is not unusual to turn toward *Lectio Divina* when we become adrift and confused about the meaning of marriage. Three specific moments come to mind:

Interpreting unexpected events in the marriage. Every couple confronts them: times of illness, major changes in occupation, losses in a family, twists of fate that shake up traditional values.

During these times of uncertainty (and we have plenty of our own) we generally turn to one of our favorite psalms and listen to the promises God makes about God's loyalty to us, like this section of Psalm 91:

> "Because you cling to me, I will deliver you;
> I will protect you because you acknowledge my name.
> You shall call upon me and I will answer you.
> I will be with you in times of trouble;
> I will deliver you and glorify you
> and show you my salvation."
>
> (Ps 91:14–16)

We have turned to this section any number of times during the last twenty years, while searching for answers to some of the complex problems of life. For most of them, we never really received a satisfactory answer about why something turned sour. We do, however, rediscover that God is unswervingly, steadfastly, intensely loyal.

Out of the darkness and uncertainty comes a renewed experience of love. God gives meaning to the questionable events in our lives by teaching us through this psalm (and others), that God offers meaning to life where none can be found.

Realigning the relationship. What marriage does not, at times, fall into serious misalignment? Couples find it difficult to sustain a spirit of compassion. They run short of resourcefulness, especially when they become fatigued, short-tempered or emotionally drained. Marriages threaten to unravel, even die.

At the center of the most painful misalignment is the refusal to forgive. It is especially difficult when couples rely solely on their own strengths.

The scriptures invite us to call upon God to help us forgive. In difficult scenarios, when forgiveness comes hard, *Lectio Divina* becomes an invitation to discover the rich ground of love that is presently out of reach.

One of the ways that we move toward forgiveness, especially if it is difficult to let go of resentments, is to read sections of the scriptures aloud to one another. In this way, we allow God's word to soften our hearts. This action paves the way to forgiveness, for it is almost impossible to hang on to resentments while we listen to the word of God.

Here are a few examples of the readings we use, taken from Luke's Gospel. Here, Jesus addresses a large crowd about the terms of discipleship:

> "But I say this to you who are listening: Love your enemies, do good to those who hate you, bless those who curse you, pray for those who treat you badly."
>
> (Lk 6:27)

> "Treat others as you would like them to treat you. If you love those who love you, what thanks can you expect? Even sinners love those who love them. And if you do good to those who do good to you, what thanks can you expect? Even sinners love those who love them."
>
> (Lk 6:32)

> "Do not judge, and you will not be judged yourselves; do not condemn, and you will not be condemned yourselves; grant pardon, and you will be pardoned. Give, and there will be gifts for you: a full measure, pressed down, shaken together, and running over, will be poured into your lap; because the amount you measure out is the amount you will be given back."
>
> (Lk 6:37–39)

By listening to a spouse read the word of God aloud, we enter into a dialogue with the God who is forgiveness. Thus, forgiveness of one another takes shape at a deep level.

Recapturing our vision. Most couples find it difficult to maintain a clear vision of what marriage means. Yet vision is so important to a solid spirituality that all other efforts to love collapse if vision is lost.

The scriptures reorient us toward a view of marriage that is grounded in the God of love. Our readings vary from favorite psalms to the four Gospels, and we measure our efforts to love against the norms offered in these readings.

We frequently turn to Matthew's Gospel, for example, and read aloud Jesus' Sermon on the Mount. As we listen to it, we reach for the newness of vision that a change of priorities brings with it. The Gospels call us to a radical rethinking about everything we are or hope to be:

> "Do not store up treasures for yourselves on earth, where moths and woodworms destroy them and thieves can break in and steal. But store up treasures for yourselves in heaven, where neither moth nor woodworms destroy them and thieves cannot break in and steal. For where your treasure is, there will be your heart also."
>
> (Mt 6:19)

The word of God transforms us as we read it. The vision that we sometimes lack due to fatigue, distractions or misdirected energy never fails to return.

Interpreting...
Four Questions

We have already described in some detail the importance of asking four standard questions that are an essential dimension of every *Lectio Divina:*

1. What does the text say in itself?
2. What is God saying to me personally through this text?
3. What do I want to say to God on the basis of this text?
4. What difference can this text make for how I live my life?

By walking through these four questions, the riches of the scriptures unfold and touch a couple in deep and practical ways. Yet there are other ways to mine these riches. Their understanding hinges on several different ways to interpret the meaning of the text itself. We call these the four levels of interpretation.

Interpreting...
Four Levels of Interpretation

Four levels of meaning to a specific text bring distinctly different insights to those who explore the scriptures:

The Literal Meaning
The Moral Meaning
The Allegorical Meaning
The Mystical Meaning

The *literal level* is simply an understanding of what the text is saying in its root or essential, form. In order to find the literal meaning, a serious exploration about the origins, focus or intention of the author is in order.

The central question to open up a literal meaning is a simple one: What is the author of the text trying to say to his audience?

By way of example, let us take a text from John's Gospel and examine it according to the four levels of interpretation:

> You did not choose me,
> no, I chose you;
> and I commissioned you
> to go out and bear fruit,
> fruit that will last;...
>
> (Jn 15:16)

This text is taken from John's account of Jesus' instructions to his disciples, spoken on the eve of the Passover. It is clear that Jesus speaks from a bold initiative as he describes his choice of them as disciples. Jesus speaks with the authority of God, so their commission represents a privileged calling. Moreover, God's choice implies a mandate for them to produce good works (to go out and to bear lasting fruit).

The *literal interpretation* of the text in this case is a simple narrative account of what happened on that Passover eve. It says nothing about anyone else except those who were gathered in the room with Jesus. The account is an historical narrative.

In order to understand the literal meaning of any scriptural text, a disciplined study is recommended. A good biblical commentary can open up an understanding of the historical context, the literary form, the language of the author and especially the intention of the author as the text was composed.

The question of how a text applies to one's personal life has no relevance for the moment, but a genuine understanding of the historical context of the scriptures is critical for any balanced spirituality. Understanding the content, the context or the intention of the author offers some assurance that a reader will not spin off into misdirected devotional tangents grounded in nothing more than an active imagination.

The second level of meaning, *the moral interpretation,* is more easily understood. It moves interpretation to the level of a personal mandate. If we look at the same text, it can be read as a general invitation to anyone who responds to the call of discipleship. We are called by God and invited to carry on the ideal of Jesus: to go out and do similar works. We can choose to respond or not respond.

Thus, a moral interpretation moves us to action. Can we take the call lightly? Do we refuse the commission to bear fruit? Do we realize what this means for a marriage?

A moral interpretation is easily understood, for it challenges us to reform our lives and *do* something. With the complex demands of married life, the mandate to do something probably sounds familiar. As *Lectio Divina* is practiced with this interpretation in mind, the couple is free to move from the text itself to the broader moral consequences of their lives. A reform of the way we live is at the core of this mode of interpretation.

Here, the text can be easily read as a challenge to the couple to bear fruit in the marriage. Perhaps it pushes them toward moral reform in the pursuit of justice. Maybe it means loving their children selflessly. No matter what specific form, the Gospel invites the couple to reform their lives.

An *allegorical* interpretation, the third level, is an invitation to put your memory to work. An allegory is a story rich in symbols, and an allegorical interpretation reads the symbols in a text and invites the reader to find a fuller meaning in what he or she reads.

Even though there are several types of allegory, for our purposes, the allegorical meaning invites us to read the text with a definite point of view.

Memory comes alive as a couple listens to the voice of Jesus: "I have chosen you." They recollect a sequence of specific incidents in which they recognize God's call in their lives. Memory reconstructs a patchwork quilt of images, symbols, impressions, events and dreams in which they recognize God's choice of them. *Lectio Divina* creates a clear picture of God's choices out of the patches, thread and images of their lives.

The fourth level of interpretation, *the mystical,* actually brings the couple into a special intimacy with God. They see God as loving and tender, and, like the image of Jesus, God invites them into close union with him. The best way to describe this level is simply that of an awareness of the presence of God in all matters. The text acts as a doorway into the real presence of God.

We especially find this style of interpretation among couples who have practiced *Lectio Divina* for a period of time. They are on such pleasant terms with God that they recognize God's presence in all actions, all dialogue with one another. The scriptures help them deepen and confirm what they know intuitively.

We hope that these brief explanations of the four levels of meaning will help open up the scriptures for you. As understanding deepens, a thoughtful reading of the scriptures will invite you into the hidden ground of love from different angles. Each mode of interpretation can act as a prism as it breaks down the sunlight into the colors of the spectrum.

Going Live Again...Once More with Feeling

"Tell us a love story," P. J. invites.

We stand once again in front of a group of thirty-five couples who have been exploring their marriages for the last twenty-four hours. They have listened, shared, dined together, laughed, weighed the heavy matters of love and found solitude in their walks in the woods. Most of them spent the night here, enjoying their first breakaway from their children in months.

The warm January sunshine fosters a feeling of lazy expectancy. Several pairs of walkers slowly file in from outside. Inside the lodge, the smell of aspen smoke invites the couples to do their final sharing about their lives, their marriages, their understanding of the hidden ground of love. By late Saturday afternoon, they are ready to sum it all up before heading back to their families.

"C'mon, someone take a risk, and tell us a love story. Share an experience of how you have grown, or what you have discovered about love," P. J. prompts.

A slight woman raises her hand, stands up, and the room quiets down.

"I want to share something," she says. "I want to share what we have learned."

"Go ahead."

"We—my husband and I—we learned a lot about one another. We have been married for nineteen years, and we have always tried to pray a little bit each morning. We always had trouble getting started, but we learned a lot the last couple of days. We tried some of that business about not saying a whole lot, just listening for the voice of God, and we felt OK. Of course, my husband liked that, because he always has a hard time thinking of something to say."

The couples laugh as her husband shifts, then smiles. She abruptly sits down, obviously finished with her message.

"Well done....Now, anyone else ready?"

No one offers anything, so we wait for what seems like a long time. Thirty seconds later, a woman, probably in her late twenties, stands up.

"This weekend has been so good for us," she says, as her voice catches a bit. "We have had a real hard time feeling much of anything lately, because the pressures of life get to us. It seems like the only thing marriage means is continued obligation. Well, this weekend we got back in touch. I'm not too sure what happened—we found that the scriptures about the treasure hidden in the field made us realize that we had been missing a great deal. We spent lots of time walking in the woods, holding hands for the first time in years, and getting back some fee...feelings."

The group visibly pulls for her to continue, feeling both her hesitation and her excitement about what happened.

"It came back. The feelings came back, and we rediscovered something we had lost."

Her husband takes to his feet, tries to speak, embraces her, and the group applauds. Then they sit down, moved by the power of their own emotions.

The stories begin to unfold easily. Each love story is a little different, but the couples identify with one another through the common themes of struggle and fulfillment.

What is most apparent is how different each couple is in their effort to sustain a vision of what marriage might be for them.

"We have been married for a long time—forty-one years,

and we have been through it all—and we still manage to find newness when we take the time to search for it," one gray-haired gentleman states. He carries himself well, obviously accustomed to speaking in front of a group.

"We have come through some mighty hard days, working like mad at times to keep this marriage alive. It really came to life when we learned to pray together. We try to do it each day. We have a solarium, and we meditate and pray as the morning sun fills the room with warmth. We have discovered one great lesson—ya gotta stay with it for a time. It seems like sometimes nothing is happening, then God just knocks us over with a pleasant surprise. We know that God sustains us and will be faithful to us to the end."

"We hope that's not too soon, though," his wife states. He smiles at her reassuringly, then sits down.

The love stories continue. Processes deepen through feeling, touching, hearing one another for the first time. At the center of each one of their stories lies the universal theme of balancing: I, you and we.

Lectio Divina:
Closure

"We have one last exercise in *Lectio Divina* for you, then we'll bring the workshop to a close. We want you to sit close to one another and listen to this reading. Claudette will read it aloud for you. Like we explained to you yesterday, listen for the four levels of interpretation: literal, moral, allegorical and mystical."

Claudette opens the scripture and begins. "This is a brief reading from the beginning of John's Gospel," she says, "I'm going to read it very slowly four times. I'll pause for a time and P. J. will ask you to spontaneously comment on its meaning. Here we go."

> The Word was made flesh,
> he lived among us,
> and we saw his glory,
> the glory that is his as the only Son of the Father,
> full of grace and truth.
>
> (Jn 1:14)

After a long pause, as the couples reflect on the text, P. J. calls for their response. "OK," he says, "someone give me a literal interpretation."

"God pitches his tent among us, becomes part of our lives," an unknown voice says.

"God becomes one of us. God invests in our struggles to be human. It has something to do with a manifestation of glory—whatever that is."

"Very good. OK Claudette, read it a second time."

> The Word was made flesh,
> he lived among us,
> and we saw his glory,
> the glory that is his as the only Son of the Father,
> full of grace and truth.

After a pause, someone begins, "A moral interpretation is easy. We are mandated to love because God first loves us.

We can't do anything without God first becoming a part of our lives."

"That sounds allegorical to me," someone says, "because the symbolism of pitching a tent with us is so real. God becomes one of us by offering hospitality. We are changed by the gesture of hospitality. I can understand that image so easily now; I know God has embraced us for the whole of our marital history."

"I give up,..." P. J. says. "You are both right because your hunger for God allows you to hear, see, feel differently. Keeping these different interpretations straight can be difficult. Let's keep our perspective alive for now and not worry too much about it. All we really ask is that you take a little time and try to build some discipline into your understanding of *Lectio Divina* by doing some honest study."

"What difference does it make?" someone asks. "The important thing is to know that God loves us first and we can love one another in return."

"I can't disagree with that," P. J. answers, "but I still insist that a disciplined understanding of the word of God keeps us from going off on a lark. Study and reflection refine our thoughts about God's love and fill our effort to love one another with wonder. Hey, I'm not talking about getting a doctorate in scripture studies. I'm talking about twenty minutes a day to take a deeper look at what is right in front of you. We're still at it, still learning so much, still discovering the richness of God's love for us."

"Listen one last time," Claudette says. "This time try to move into the mystical level. Listen more with your hearts. It is actually the easiest of all the modes if you allow your hearts to open."

The Word was made flesh,
he lived among us,
and we saw his glory,
the glory that is his as the only Son of The Father,
full of grace and truth.

There is a long pause this time, a full three minutes as the *Lectio Divina* does its work. Most of the couples have their eyes closed, or they look lost in reflection. The responses begin to flow like living water from rich subterranean sources.

"God is, God loves, God lives in our union."

"He pitches his tent in our hearts, embraces us with warm hospitality and invites us to stay forever."

"We see his glory every time we try to love a little more selflessly."

"God is holy ground, God is foundation. God is love."

Then it becomes very quiet, this time lasting for a full five minutes, but there is no anxiety, no restlessness, no attempts to break the silence. We see couples join hands, gently reassuring one another about their presence through affectionate squeezes. Others keep a respectful space between them.

The intricate terrain of the hidden ground of love and its unique geography for each couple evolves into an accepted silence. We know that deep within them rich encounters with Love continue the work of genuine transformation.

Epilogue

We have made an effort to blend *Lectio Divina* and couple process in order to create a view of marital spirituality as an entry into the hidden ground of love.

To our knowledge, this is the first serious joining of these seemingly diverse realities, and we hope that our efforts will encourage others to make similar efforts.

Marital spirituality as a legitimate form of the spiritual quest is an idea whose time has come. In order to speak to contemporary couples, we suggest it must be grounded upon these foundations:

- the lived experience of marriage
- a solid foundation in scripture
- a trustworthy method of prayerfulness
- a healthy marital process
- an emphasis on wholeness

Continued dialogue with married couples convinces us that God is alive in their efforts to love. By encouraging them to speak about their experiences, they share from the abundance of God's gifts to them. Each statement they make somehow furthers a developing sophistication of what marital spirituality means. We hope that our efforts contribute to the final outcome.

Notes

1. M. Basil Pennington, *Lectio Divina: Renewing the Ancient Practice of Praying the Scriptures* (New York: Crossroad, 1998), ix.

2. Ibid., 125.

3. Michael Casey, *Sacred Reading: The Ancient Art of Lectio Divina* (Liguori, Missouri: Triumph Books, 1995), vi.

4. Ibid., 8–9.

5. Wilkie Au and Noreen Cannon, *Urgings of The Heart: A Spirituality of Integration* (Mahwah, N. J.: Paulist Press, 1995), 10.

6. Ernest S. Wolf, M.D., *Treating the Self: Elements of Clinical Self-Psychology* (New York: Guilford Press, 1988), 27.

7. Michael Casey, *Toward God: The Ancient Wisdom of Western Prayer* (Liguori, Missouri: Triumph Books, 1989), 61.

8. Ibid., 13.

9. William H. Shannon, *Silence On Fire: The Prayer of Awareness* (New York: Crossroad, 1991), 23.

10. Evelyn Eaton Whitehead and James D. Whitehead, *A Sense of Sexuality* (New York: Doubleday, 1989), 208.

11. Sam Keen, *To Love and Be Loved* (New York: Bantam Books, 1997), 206.

12. Ibid., 4.

13. Herbert Benson, M.D., *Timeless Healing* (New York: Simon and Schuster, 1996), 17.

14. Ibid., 197–198.

15. William H. Shannon, *Something of a Rebel: Thomas Merton His Life and Works* (Cincinnati, Ohio: St. Anthony Messenger Press, 1997), 67.

16. Thomas Merton, *New Seeds of Contemplation* (New York: New Directions, 1961), 41.

17. Thomas Merton, *The Hidden Ground of Love,* ed. William H. Shannon (New York: Farrar, Strauss, Giroux, 1985), 115.

18. Ibid., 115.

19. Ibid., 115.

20. Sam Keen, op. cit., 40.

21. Judith S. Wallerstein and Sandra Blakeslee, *The Good Marriage* (New York: Houghton Mifflin, 1995), 13.

22. Ibid., 13.

23 Ibid., 62–63.

24. John Welwood, Ph.D., *Journey of The Heart* (New York: HarperCollins, 1990), 207.

25. John Welwood, *Love and Awakening* (New York: HarperCollins, 1996), xiii.

26. Thomas Merton, *Learning to Love: The Journals of Thomas Merton,* ed. Christine M. Bochen (San Francisco: HarperCollins, 1997), 40.

27. Sam Keen, op. cit., 5.

28. Frank X. Tuoti, *Why Not Be a Mystic?* (New York: Crossroad, 1995), 25.

29. William Shannon, *Silence on Fire*, 22.

30. Frank X. Tuoti, op. cit., 21.

31. Ibid., 26.

32. Thomas Merton, *New Seeds of Contemplation*, 1.

33. William Shannon, *Silence on Fire*, 23.

34. Willigis Jäger, *The Way To Contemplation* (Mahwah, N. J.: Paulist Press, 1982), 55.

35. Thomas Merton, *New Seeds of Contemplation*, 13.

36. Mary Brian Durkin, O.P., "Evelyn Underhill's Guidelines for a Sane Spiritual Life," *Spiritual Life* (winter 1997): 239.

37. Willigis Jäger, op. cit., 55.

38. Andrew Weil, M.D., *Spontaneous Healing,* (New York: Ballantine, 1995), 204.

39. Ibid., 205.

40. William Shannon, *Silence on Fire*, 41–42.

41. Thomas Merton, *The Hidden Ground of Love*, 63–64.

42. Herbert Benson, *Timeless Healing*, 134.

43. Ibid.

44. Thomas Keating, *Intimacy With God* (New York: Crossroad, 1994), 64.

45. Thich Nhat Hanh, *The Miracle of Mindfulness* (Boston: Beacon Press, 1975), 131.

46. The Jerusalem Bible, 14.

47. Michael Casey, *Sacred Reading,* 9.

48. Ibid., 80.

49. Ibid., 48.

50. Michael Casey, *Toward God: The Ancient Wisdom of Western Prayer,* 73.

51. Ibid., 108.

52. Michael Casey, *Sacred Reading,* 100.

Also by Patrick J. and Claudette M. McDonald
published by Paulist Press

Out of the Ashes: A Handbook for Starting Over